The Forgotten Profession

Restoring Humanity to Insurance

By Steven R. Wiatrek

The Forgotten Profession: Restoring Humanity to Insurance

ISBN: 979-8-9949192-1-7

Published by The Wiatrek Group, LLC
Poth, Texas, USA

This book represents the personal opinions, experiences, and
observations of the author. It is not intended as legal, financial,
or professional advice. The views expressed are solely those of
the author and do not reflect those of any past, present, or
future employer, business partner, or affiliate.

Printed in the United States of America
First Edition – 2026

<u>DEDICATION</u>

This book is dedicated to my community and to the people I have been entrusted to serve.

To the families who invited me to their kitchen tables. To the neighbors who trusted me with their questions, their worries, and their futures. To the farmers, small business owners, parents, and retirees who reminded me that this work is never about policies alone.

It is dedicated to those who taught me—often without knowing it— that trust is built slowly, that words carry weight, and that showing up still matters.

To the quiet professionals who do this work with integrity, who choose patience over pressure, and who understand that protecting people is a responsibility, not a transaction.

And to the communities that raised me, shaped me, and continue to hold me accountable— this book exists because of you.

This kind of work demands more than competence.

<u>Author's Note:</u>

This book was not written out of anger.

It was written out of concern.

After years in the insurance profession—after kitchen tables, late-night phone calls, renewals, losses, rebuilds, and quiet wins—I began to notice something unsettling. Not in the policies. Not in the products.

But in the posture of the work.

Salesmanship, as a craft, was changing. And not always for the better.

I watched capable, intelligent professionals move faster than they listened. I saw conversations shortened, pressure normalized, and relationships treated as transactions. I heard words like quota, production, conversion, and volume spoken far more often than trust, responsibility, or stewardship.

The work was still being done.

But the weight of it felt lighter.

And that worried me.

This is the third book in a longer conversation I did not originally intend to have.

My first book focused on the practice of insurance sales—the mechanics, discipline, and mindset required to succeed honestly. It was written to help professionals do the work well.

My second book was more personal. It explored identity, resilience, faith, and the cost of starting over. It was written to help professionals remember why they work.

This book exists because something was still missing.

It asks a deeper question:

What happens when a profession forgets what it was built to protect?

Insurance is not neutral work.

It shows up at moments of vulnerability—death, loss, uncertainty, rebuilding. It intersects with fear, responsibility, and hope. It often involves people making decisions they never wanted to face.

This kind of work demands more than competence.

x

Table Of Contents

Introduction: Where Trust Was Learned Before It Was Sold

If you grow up in a small town, you learn early that the world is not held together by rules or regulations.

It is held together by people.

Quiet, ordinary, dependable people who treat promises like sacred things.

Long before I ever understood the word insurance, I understood its spirit.

I saw it in the way neighbors showed up without being asked when a storm tore a roof from a home. I saw it in casseroles delivered to grieving families before the sun rose. I saw it in farmers who loaned equipment with nothing more than a nod. I saw it in handshakes exchanged in the pews of a modest country church, where a man's word still carried weight.

Back then, trust was not a luxury.

It was the currency of life.

Every Saturday, my father would take me into town to run errands. These trips were never rushed. There was no checklist to complete and no clock dictating the pace. Town had its own rhythm, and you moved within it whether you planned to or not.

The postmaster knew which families were waiting on letters and which ones were hoping they wouldn't come. The banker didn't sit behind glass. He stepped out from behind his desk and asked questions that had nothing to do with money and everything to do with people. The grocer asked how the harvest was holding up that year—not out of politeness, but because he understood what a bad season meant for a family.

People talked slowly. They lingered. They asked questions and waited for real answers.

No one called it relationship building.

It was simply how life worked.

I didn't know it then, but those mornings were teaching me something that would take years to name: trust is formed long before it is tested.

By the time someone needed help, the relationship was already there.

I did not grow up thinking about insurance.

I grew up watching how adults handled responsibility.

I watched how they showed up when something went wrong. How they spoke carefully when decisions carried consequence. How they avoided promises they weren't sure they could keep—and honored the ones they made, even when it cost them.

I learned that reputation wasn't something you claimed. It was something you were given—slowly, carefully, and conditionally.

And once given, it had to be protected.

Insurance, in its earliest form, belonged to places like this.

It was born in communities where people knew one another's names, histories, and burdens. It emerged not from strategy, but from necessity. From the simple conviction that no neighbor should face catastrophe alone.

Insurance was never meant to be abstract.

It was meant to be personal.

Over time, the world changed.

It grew louder. Faster. More efficient.

Technology shortened distances. Systems replaced memory. Processes replaced presence.

Much of this progress was necessary.

But something subtle was lost along the way.

The work became lighter.

This book is about restoring weight.

It is about remembering what the work requires.

It is about choosing depth over speed, responsibility over convenience, and humanity over efficiency.

Let us begin there.

"Somewhere along the way, we took a detour in this profession. The good news is….we can still get back to doing it the right way."

Steven R. Wiatrek

CHAPTER 1: When Insurance Still Had a Soul

Where Trust Was Learned Before It Was Named

If you grow up in a small town, you learn early that the world is not held together by rules or

regulations.

It is held together by people.

Quiet, ordinary, dependable people who treat promises like sacred things.

Long before I ever understood the word insurance, I understood its spirit—though I would not have

called it that at the time.

I saw it in the way neighbors showed up without being asked when a storm tore a roof from a home. I

saw it in casseroles delivered to grieving families before the sun rose. I saw it in farmers who loaned

equipment with nothing more than a nod, trusting it would come back because it always had. I saw it in

handshakes exchanged in places where a man's word still carried weight long after the conversation

ended.

Back then, trust was not discussed.

It was assumed.

It was not marketed.

It was not optimized.

It was not tracked, measured, or analyzed.

It was lived.

Every Saturday, my father would take me into town to run errands. These trips were never rushed.

There was no checklist dictating the pace and no urgency to "get through it." Town had its own

rhythm, and you moved within it whether you planned to or not.

What I didn't understand then—but recognize clearly now—is that those errands were never just

errands.

They were lessons.

The postmaster knew which families were waiting on letters—and which ones were hoping they

wouldn't come. The banker didn't hide behind a desk or a screen. He stepped out, asked questions,

and listened in a way that suggested he actually cared about the answers. The grocer didn't ask about

the harvest out of politeness. He asked because he understood what a bad season meant—not just for

income, but for an entire family's stability.

People talked slowly.

They lingered.

They asked questions—and more importantly, they waited for real answers.

There was no script.

No funnel.

No urgency to close anything.

No one called it relationship building.

It was simply how life worked.

I didn't know it then, but those mornings were teaching me something that would take years to fully

understand and even longer to articulate:

Trust is formed long before it is tested.

By the time someone needed help, the relationship was already there.

That mattered more than anything that could be written in a contract.

Because when something went wrong—and eventually, something always did—people didn't turn to

systems first.

They turned to people they already knew.

Before Protection Was Outsourced

Insurance, in its earliest form, did not begin with contracts, policies, or applications.

It began with responsibility.

Before insurance had language, it had expectation.

Before it had structure, it had conscience.

Before it had pricing, it had participation.

In the early days of American life, protection was not something you purchased.

It was something you belonged to.

Communities were small, not by design, but by necessity. People lived close enough to one another that

absence was noticed immediately. A door left unopened too long raised concern. A missed Sunday

service did not go unnoticed. A quiet house meant something had gone wrong.

Life was fragile in ways that are difficult to fully appreciate today.

Work was dangerous. Illness arrived without warning. Medical care was limited. Travel was slow.

Communication was inconsistent. There were no systems waiting in the background to stabilize a

household when something went wrong.

And when a working man died, it did not simply end a life.

It destabilized everything.

His labor was not supplemental income.

It was the income.

When it disappeared, the household did not gradually adjust.

It unraveled.

Rent did not wait.

Food did not stretch indefinitely.

Winter did not soften its demands.

There were no safety nets. No government programs quietly stepping in. No policies to file or claims to process.

When tragedy struck, the question was not:

"What coverage do we have?"

It was:

Will anyone come?

And that question was not theoretical.

It was immediate.

And it was deeply uncertain.

Sometimes help came quickly.

Sometimes it came slowly.

And sometimes, it did not come at all.

But when it did come, it came with faces attached.

It came with people who knew your name, your situation, your family.

And when it didn't come, the absence was visible.

That visibility shaped behavior.

People understood that their choices—what they promised, how they showed up, whether they

followed through—would not remain hidden.

Reputation was not something you claimed.

It was something you were given.

Slowly. Carefully. And conditionally.

Protection, in that world, was not transactional.

It was relational.

And because it was relational, it carried weight.

When Communities Chose to Act Before Loss

Over time, communities began to recognize a hard truth:

Reacting after loss was not enough.

Sympathy, no matter how sincere, arrived too late to prevent damage. Charity, no matter how generous,

was inconsistent. Good intentions could not be relied upon when survival was at stake.

So something began to shift.

Not dramatically. Not all at once.

But intentionally.

Communities moved from reaction to preparation.

Small contributions were set aside regularly. Not large amounts. Not anything that would draw

attention. Just enough to matter when it mattered most.

These were not premiums.

They were pledges.

A quiet agreement among people who understood that one day, the roles could reverse.

I may not need this today—but I accept that one day I might.

This was the foundation of mutual aid.

And it was built on humility.

No one stood above the system.

No one was immune from risk.

No one was exempt from responsibility.

Participation was not optional—it was expected.

In many communities, these systems were simple but disciplined.

Funds were collected regularly.

They were safeguarded carefully.

And when loss occurred, they were delivered quickly.

There were no long delays.

No extended evaluations.

No process designed to question whether the loss was "valid enough."

Loss itself was proof.

One of the clearest examples of this model can be seen in early parish-based aid systems and fraternal

organizations.

Groups of men would contribute small amounts into a shared fund. When one of them died, that fund

would be delivered directly to his family—often within days.

Not months.

Days.

The purpose was not to replace a lifetime of income.

It was to preserve stability.

To keep a family in their home long enough to think clearly.

To keep food on the table long enough to avoid immediate desperation.

To keep children with their mother long enough to prevent irreversible decisions.

The money was not large.

But it was immediate.

And that immediacy mattered more than the amount.

Because delay, in those moments, was as damaging as absence.

Organizations like the Knights of Columbus eventually formalized these systems, but the idea itself

was not new.

It had already been proven at the community level.

Protection works best when it is built in advance—and honored without hesitation.

Not as charity.

But as obligation.

When Distance Entered the Work

Over time, the world expanded.

Communities grew.

Systems developed.

Technology advanced.

Efficiency became possible in ways earlier generations could not have imagined.

And much of that progress was necessary.

It allowed protection to reach more people.

It created consistency where there had once been uncertainty.

It stabilized systems that had previously depended on memory and proximity.

But progress introduced something else.

Distance.

Responsibility, once held closely, began to spread outward. Tasks were divided. Roles were

specialized. Decisions were made farther from the people they affected.

And with that distance, something subtle began to change.

The work became lighter.

Not easier.

Lighter.

The person making the recommendation was no longer always present when it was tested. The person

approving the decision was not always the one who would see the outcome. The system

functioned—but the connection between decision and consequence weakened.

And when consequence softens, behavior shifts.

Not because people become less ethical.

But because the system no longer requires the same level of care.

The work continues.

Policies are written.

Coverage is issued.

Claims are processed.

Systems operate efficiently.

But the posture changes.

What was once a shared responsibility becomes a managed process.

What was once a promise begins to resemble a product.

What was once deeply personal becomes increasingly transactional.

And over time, that shift becomes normal.

So normal that it is rarely questioned.

This book exists because of that normalization.

Not to reject progress.

Not to dismantle systems.

Not to argue that the past should be recreated exactly as it was.

But to ask a necessary question:

What happens when a profession forgets what it was built to protect?

Because insurance, at its core, is not neutral work.

It shows up in moments people cannot predict.

It intersects with fear, responsibility, and uncertainty.

It requires individuals and families to make decisions they often do not fully understand.

And that kind of work demands more than efficiency.

It demands judgment.

It demands presence.

It demands restraint.

And above all—

It demands trust.

"Well Done is better than well said"

Benjamin Franklin

Chapter 2: Pennies for the Widow

Where Protection Became Tangible

The idea that would become insurance did not begin with policies or paperwork.

It began with coins.

Not many of them. Not impressive amounts. Just enough to matter at the moment it mattered most.

After generations of watching families unravel, communities reached a quiet conclusion: waiting until tragedy arrived was too late.

Sympathy was not a strategy. Charity was inconsistent. Good intentions arrived unevenly and often after damage had already been done.

What families needed was certainty.

They needed to know—before loss arrived—that help would come.

So the earliest forms of protection took shape in the most unremarkable way imaginable: small, regular contributions set aside with discipline and purpose.

A few pennies at a time.

Why the Amount Didn't Matter

What mattered was not how much was given.

It was when it was given.

The contributions were intentionally modest so that no one was excluded. Participation mattered more than capacity. A man did not need wealth to belong—only willingness.

Each contribution said the same thing:

I may not be the one who needs this today, but I accept that one day I might be.

This was the humility at the center of mutual aid.

No one stood above the system. No one was immune from risk. No one was exempt from responsibility.

The pennies mattered because they were given in advance—before emotion, before urgency, before desperation could distort judgment.

They were given calmly, faithfully, and without spectacle.

The Widow Was Not an Abstraction

In early communities, widows were not theoretical examples.

They were known by name.

Everyone knew which families were most vulnerable. Everyone understood which households depended entirely on one income. Everyone recognized the signs of collapse when they appeared.

This familiarity shaped the system.

The purpose of early protection was not to preserve lifestyle. It was to preserve structure.

To keep families intact long enough for stability to return. To prevent children from being scattered. To prevent grief from being compounded by separation and shame.

The pennies collected were not meant to replace a lifetime of income.

They were meant to buy time.

Time to breathe. Time to adjust. Time to decide what came next without hunger forcing the answer.

When the Coins Were Delivered

When death arrived, the exchange was quiet.

There were no speeches. No signatures. No ceremony.

A knock at the door. A small envelope. A few words spoken softly, if at all.

The widow did not have to explain her situation. Everyone already knew it. She did not have to prove need. Loss itself was proof enough.

The money was not large, but it was immediate.

It paid the rent that month. It kept food on the table. It prevented the first irreversible decision from being made too soon.

Most importantly, it arrived without humiliation.

She did not receive charity.

She received what had been promised.

That distinction mattered more than any dollar amount ever could.

Why Speed Was Everything

The most important feature of early mutual aid was not generosity.

It was speed.

Delay destroyed households as effectively as absence.

Rent deadlines did not pause for grief. Grocers could not extend credit indefinitely. Winter did not wait.

Because the money had already been collected, it could be delivered without debate. There were no committees to convene. No approvals to seek. No judgments to pass.

The promise had already been made.

And because it had been made in advance, it did not depend on mood, visibility, or sympathy.

It depended on obligation.

Obligation Over Charity

These early contributions were never framed as charity.

Charity flows downward. Obligation flows outward.

Charity allows the giver to decide when help is deserved. Obligation removes that discretion. Once the promise is made, it must be honored.

This mutual dependence fostered discipline.

Funds were guarded carefully. Claims were honored quickly but honestly. Abuse was rare not because rules were strict, but because proximity discouraged dishonesty.

Everyone knew one another. Everyone knew what loss looked like.

The Quiet Dignity of the Exchange

The absence of spectacle was intentional.

Aid delivered with fanfare would have defeated its purpose. The goal was preservation, not publicity. To help without shaming. To support without diminishing dignity.

Because no single person stood above the widow as benefactor, dignity was preserved on both sides.

This is why the system endured.

Why This Was Revolutionary

What made this approach revolutionary was not innovation.

It was restraint.

Early mutual aid resisted the temptation to moralize loss. There were no interrogations of worthiness. No evaluations of effort. No conditions placed on grief.

Death was understood as inevitable—not as failure.

The system existed to respond to reality, not to judge it.

The First Line Drawn in Advance

In effect, these early systems drew a line in advance and said:

When loss crosses this line, response is automatic.

That line mattered.

It transformed help from a favor into a function. It removed uncertainty at the moment uncertainty was most destructive.

This is the origin of insurance at its most honest.

Not a transaction. A covenant.

Not a product. A promise.

From Good Intentions to Guardrails

Once communities accepted that protection had to exist before loss arrived, a new problem emerged—one that could not be solved with goodwill alone.

Good intentions were powerful, but they were fragile.

Mutual aid depended entirely on trust, and trust could be broken far more easily than it could be built. A system that promised certainty could not afford inconsistency. A single failure—one delayed response, one missing contribution, one broken promise—had the potential to undo years of discipline.

Early communities understood this instinctively.

If pennies were going to matter, they had to be protected.

So what began as informal contribution slowly evolved into careful stewardship. Rules were not introduced to restrict generosity, but to preserve it. Structure did not appear because people were greedy. It appeared because people were human.

Money—even in small amounts—changes behavior. Without clarity, funds could be delayed, redirected, or quietly depleted. Communities learned quickly that if protection was to remain reliable, it could not rely on memory or assumption.

It required guardrails.

Why Structure Became Necessary

The earliest forms of structure were simple, but intentional.

Expectations were defined clearly so that no one could claim confusion when responsibility arrived.

Who could participate. How often contributions were made. Where the funds were kept. When aid was released. Who was responsible for overseeing the process.

These decisions were not bureaucratic exercises. They were acts of preservation.

Participation meant responsibility. Belonging meant accountability.

If you contributed, you accepted the rules. If you received aid, you did so without shame—but also without entitlement beyond what had been promised.

This balance mattered.

Without structure, generosity became uneven. With too much structure, compassion risked becoming rigid. The goal was not control. The goal was continuity.

Stewardship Over Control

Those entrusted with overseeing early funds were chosen carefully—and rarely eagerly.

They were not selected for ambition or influence. They were chosen for reputation. For steadiness. For restraint. Often, they were the men least interested in authority.

These stewards understood something essential:

They did not own the money. They did not control the promise.

Their role was custodial, not authoritative.

They were responsible for ensuring that aid arrived as promised—on time, intact, and without favoritism. They did not decide who deserved help. That decision had already been made collectively by participation itself.

This distinction protected the system from ego.

Transparency was expected. Records were kept—not to audit morality, but to preserve memory. Everyone knew where the funds were. Everyone knew how they moved. Everyone knew when they were released.

Visibility prevented abuse long before enforcement was needed.

Why Abuse Was Rare—but Treated Seriously

Abuse did occur occasionally. It was inevitable.

But when it did, it was addressed swiftly and directly—not because money was sacred, but because trust was.

One misuse threatened the entire structure. If confidence eroded, contributions would stop. And if contributions stopped, the promise dissolved.

Early communities did not respond to misuse with immediate punishment. They responded with clarity. Expectations were restated. Boundaries reinforced. Restoration was preferred whenever possible.

Only when dishonesty persisted did exclusion occur.

This approach preserved participation without breeding fear.

The goal was never to shame. The goal was to protect the promise.

Mutual Aid as Shared Risk

One of the most misunderstood aspects of early mutual aid is how deeply risk was shared.

Contributors did not view their pennies as donations. They viewed them as deposits into a collective future. Each man understood that his own household might one day stand in need of the same help.

This awareness created humility.

No one contributed as a benefactor. No one received as a supplicant.

Everyone stood on equal ground.

This is why hierarchy was resisted. Titles were functional, not aspirational. Authority was temporary and limited. Decisions were made collectively whenever possible.

Mutual aid worked because it preserved equality at the moment of greatest vulnerability.

The Tension Between Compassion and Sustainability

As mutual aid systems grew, communities encountered a difficult tension—one that remains relevant today.

Compassion pulled toward generosity. Sustainability demanded restraint.

If aid was too generous, funds depleted quickly. If it was too limited, families remained at risk. Finding balance required patience, discipline, and difficult conversations.

These conversations were rarely comfortable.

How much was enough? How often could aid be given? What obligations remained after the initial support arrived?

There were no perfect answers.

But the willingness to ask these questions honestly distinguished mutual aid from charity. Charity avoided limits because limits felt unkind. Mutual aid embraced limits because limits preserved the system.

This discipline allowed protection to endure beyond isolated events.

When Expectation Replaced Hope

Perhaps the most important transformation occurred when expectation replaced hope.

Hope is fragile. Expectation is stabilizing.

Once communities trusted that aid would arrive as promised, behavior changed. Families planned differently. Fear lessened. Panic subsided. Decisions were made with more clarity because they were not being forced by immediate threat.

This stability had ripple effects.

Widows could remain in their homes longer. Children stayed together more often. Communities recovered more quickly from loss.

Mutual aid did not eliminate hardship—but it reduced chaos.

That reduction mattered.

The First Signs of Formalization

As these systems proved effective, they spread.

What worked in one parish was adopted by another. What preserved families in one town was replicated in the next. Ideas traveled through work, worship, and word of mouth.

Patterns emerged.

Standard contribution amounts. Defined response timelines. Clear stewardship roles.

Consistency followed.

Communities began to recognize that mutual aid could be scalable without losing its soul—if it remained grounded in obligation rather than profit.

This realization marked the threshold between informal protection and institutional possibility.

Why This Matters

Before insurance became an industry, it was a discipline.

A discipline of foresight. A discipline of restraint. A discipline of shared responsibility.

The pennies mattered not because of their amount, but because of what they represented: a commitment made in advance, guarded carefully, and honored without hesitation.

This chapter is not nostalgia.

It is instruction.

Because the moment protection forgets why discipline exists, it becomes fragile again. And when discipline erodes, promises become suggestions.

When Protection Outgrew the Room

Mutual aid worked—sometimes so well that it created pressures its earliest architects never anticipated.

As families stabilized and communities began to recover more quickly from loss, word spread. What preserved widows in one parish caught the attention of the next. Men talked at work sites and factories. Priests exchanged ideas quietly. Families relocated and carried the model with them, not as theory, but as lived experience.

A system that kept children with their mothers did not remain unnoticed.

Soon, what had once fit comfortably inside a single room— administered by people who knew one another by name—began to outgrow its original boundaries.

More participants meant more responsibility. More families meant more claims. More claims meant more coordination.

What had once been managed through proximity now required consistency across distance.

This was not a failure of the system.

It was proof of its success.

Why Scale Became Unavoidable

The early leaders of mutual aid did not pursue growth for ambition's sake. They pursued reliability. As participation increased, the consequences of failure multiplied. A delayed response no longer affected one household—it undermined confidence across an entire community.

Without scale, protection became uneven.

One parish responded immediately. Another hesitated. One steward acted with care. Another struggled under volume.

The promise—once uniform—began to depend on who administered it.

This inconsistency threatened everything mutual aid was meant to prevent.

So the question changed.

It was no longer whether to organize more formally.

It became how to do so without losing the soul of the work.

From Stewardship to Administration

The shift that followed was subtle but profound.

Stewardship had been relational. Administration was procedural.

Stewards knew the families personally. They had stood in their kitchens. They knew which children were most vulnerable and which widows had already sold what little they owned.

Administrators, by contrast, managed systems designed to serve families they might never meet.

This distance was not chosen casually. It was imposed by necessity.

Memory gave way to records. Discretion gave way to rules. Presence gave way to process.

These changes made protection scalable. They ensured consistency across geography. They reduced favoritism and confusion.

They also made protection abstract.

The person approving aid was no longer always present when it was received. The decision no longer carried the same emotional weight.

That mattered.

The First Moral Trade-Off

This was the first true moral trade-off in the evolution of insurance.

Efficiency improved. Reach expanded. Reliability increased.

But intimacy declined.

A decision made in an office did not carry the same gravity as one made at a kitchen table. A rule applied universally could not account for every nuance of grief. What had once been guided by conscience was now guided by criteria.

This shift was not malicious.

It was structural.

And structure always reshapes responsibility.

Why Rules Replaced Judgment

As systems grew, judgment became dangerous.

Judgment invited bias. Bias invited resentment. Resentment fractured participation.

Rules were introduced not to remove compassion, but to protect fairness. They ensured that help was not dependent on persuasion, personality, or familiarity. They reduced the emotional burden on those tasked with administering aid.

But rules also created distance.

A widow no longer faced a neighbor who knew her story. She faced a process designed to treat her fairly among many.

Fairness replaced familiarity.

This was progress—and loss—at the same time.

The Emergence of Professional Roles

As institutions expanded, roles began to specialize.

Some people collected contributions. Others managed records. Others approved distributions.

Over time, these roles demanded skill, consistency, and time. Eventually, they demanded compensation.

This was another turning point.

The work that had once been carried voluntarily now required full-time attention. Paying administrators was not a betrayal of purpose—it was an acknowledgment of reality.

But compensation changed perception.

When people are paid to administer protection, questions arise.

Are they serving the mission—or the role? Are decisions guided by conscience—or compliance? Is restraint still possible when growth rewards expansion?

These questions did not surface immediately. But they were inevitable.

When Distance Became Normal

As generations passed, institutional distance became normalized.

Most participants no longer remembered the fragility that had birthed the system. They inherited stability without witnessing collapse. Protection became expected rather than cherished.

This altered posture.

Contributions felt less like obligation and more like dues. Aid felt less like preservation and more like entitlement. The system continued to function—but the emotional weight lightened.

This is not condemnation.

It is consequence.

When protection works long enough, people forget why it exists.

The Quiet Shift in Language

Language shifted alongside structure.

Promises became benefits. Obligations became coverage. Participation became membership.

These changes were subtle, but they mattered.

Language shapes posture. When protection is described in transactional terms, it is treated transactionally. What had once been a covenant now resembled a service.

This did not happen because people stopped caring.

It happened because systems succeeded.

Standing at the Threshold

Chapter two stands at a threshold.

Behind us is a world where pennies preserved families because people stood close enough to feel the consequence of failure.

Ahead lies a world where protection becomes professionalized, efficient, and scalable—but also vulnerable to drift.

The question is not whether scale was necessary.

It was.

The question is whether conscience survived the transition intact.

That question belongs to the final section of this chapter.

When the Promise Became a Product

Institutions solved problems that mutual aid could not.

They stabilized response. They expanded reach. They standardized protection across distance and time.

And in doing so, they made something else possible.

They made protection sustainable beyond memory.

But sustainability came with consequence.

Once protection could be administered at scale, it could also be priced. Once it could be priced, it could be measured. And once it could be measured, it could be optimized.

This was the moment the promise began to change shape.

Not because the intention was wrong. But because incentives entered the room.

The Introduction of Profit

Profit did not arrive as a villain.

It arrived as a solution.

Institutions required buildings, staff, systems, and reserves. People administering protection needed compensation. Funds needed to be managed responsibly. Growth required capital.

Profit, at first, was simply the margin required to keep the system functioning.

But margins have gravity.

Once profit exists, it demands attention. Once it is measured, it becomes a target. Once it becomes a target, behavior shifts—slowly at first, then decisively.

The question subtly changes.

Not "Is the promise being honored?" But "Is the system performing?"

Performance metrics replaced lived consequence.

Incentives Quietly Rewriting Behavior

In early mutual aid, incentives were moral.

If you failed, you saw the result. If you delayed, families suffered visibly. If you promised carelessly, you bore the cost personally.

Distance had protected institutions from chaos—but it also insulated them from consequence.

Now, decisions were judged not by impact on a household, but by alignment with policy, margin, and efficiency. Protection was no longer evaluated at the kitchen table. It was evaluated on spreadsheets.

This did not require malice.

It required distance.

When incentives reward growth, expansion becomes virtue. When expansion becomes virtue, restraint begins to look like inefficiency. When restraint disappears, promises stretch thinner than they were meant to go.

When Language Fully Shifted

By the time protection became a product, language had already paved the way.

Widows became claimants. Families became policyholders. Promises became coverage.

These words did not remove care—but they changed posture.

A claimant is processed. A policyholder is serviced. Coverage is adjudicated.

The system did not ask whether dignity was preserved. It asked whether rules were followed.

The Agent's Role Changes

Once, the agent was a guardian of the promise.

Now, the agent increasingly became a distributor of products.

The work was no longer anchored solely in consequence. It was anchored in quota, performance, and growth.

This did not happen overnight.

It happened one incentive at a time.

The Cost of Optimization

Optimization improves systems.

It reduces waste. It increases speed. It lowers cost.

But optimization also removes friction.

Friction forced pause. Pause forced reflection. Reflection forced restraint.

When friction disappears, decisions accelerate. Listening declines. Protection becomes transactional.

The system works.

But the soul thins.

What Was Lost—and What Remains

Much was gained.

More families protected. More stability delivered. More certainty created.

The problem is not that institutions exist.

The problem is that institutions forgot why they were built.

Yet traces of the original promise remain.

They live in agents who slow down. They live in professionals who choose restraint. They live in people who still feel the weight.

The Line That Must Be Redrawn

Every profession reaches a moment when it must decide what it serves.

Insurance has reached that moment again.

It can optimize protection as a transaction. Or it can recover its original posture.

Not by dismantling institutions. Not by rejecting progress.

But by reintroducing conscience.

Why This Chapter Matters

Pennies for the widow became systems for the masses. Systems became industries. Industries began to serve metrics.

Understanding this arc matters.

The Bridge Forward

The modern agent stands between vocation and transaction.

The question is not whether you can sell.

The question is whether you can still serve.

Because systems do not choose conscience.

People do.

"Quality is never an accident. It is always the result of intelligent effort."

John Ruskin

Chapter 3: When the Work Lost Its Weight

There was no announcement when it happened.

No memo. No training session. No official declaration that the work had changed.

One day, insurance was still a responsibility carried with gravity.

And then, quietly, it became a job.

The kind of job measured in numbers. Tracked by dashboards. Rewarded by volume.

The work did not suddenly become unethical. That is not the story. It became lighter. And when work loses its weight, behavior changes—even when intentions remain good.

Most agents did not notice the shift immediately because it did not arrive as loss. It arrived as efficiency.

Processes improved. Technology advanced. Access expanded.

Applications became easier. Quotes came faster. Signatures required fewer steps. The system became simpler to navigate, easier to scale, and more forgiving of speed.

These changes were celebrated—and rightly so. They allowed protection to reach more people than ever before.

But something else happened at the same time.

The agent became further removed from consequence.

Distance as a Feature, Not a Bug

Modern insurance systems are designed to absorb impact.

If a claim is delayed, the agent does not sit in the living room while a family waits. If coverage fails, the agent does not watch a kitchen table fall silent. If expectations are misunderstood, the system explains it away with language, exclusions, and fine print.

Distance protects the professional.

And protection from consequence feels like progress—until it reshapes posture.

When consequence disappears, urgency shifts. The work no longer demands patience; it rewards speed. It no longer requires listening; it rewards throughput. It no longer asks for restraint; it rewards volume.

This is not because agents stopped caring.

It is because the system stopped requiring them to.

The Rise of the Metric

Once consequence was removed, metrics rushed in to fill the vacuum.

Metrics are not inherently harmful. They create visibility. They allow comparison. They help organizations understand performance at scale.

But metrics also simplify reality.

A policy written becomes a win. A premium bound becomes success. A close becomes proof of value.

What metrics cannot measure is suitability. They cannot measure understanding. They cannot measure the quiet decision not to sell.

Those decisions—the restrained ones—do not show up on dashboards. They do not generate applause. They do not move rankings.

So over time, they are quietly discouraged.

A Familiar Modern Scene

Picture a modern agent late on a Friday.

Quota is close but not quite met. The pipeline is thin. The pressure is subtle but constant.

A prospect hesitates—not because they cannot afford the coverage, but because they do not fully understand it. There is time to slow down. There is time to explain. There is time to uncover what actually matters.

But there is also a number on a screen.

The agent knows the policy will likely never be tested. The risk feels distant. The system approves the application. The commission posts immediately.

Nothing feels wrong.

And yet, something feels off.

That unease is not incompetence. It is not burnout. It is not lack of motivation.

It is weightlessness.

When the Agent Was No Longer the Last Line

There was a time when the agent knew—deep down—that once the paperwork was signed, they were still on the hook.

They would get the call. They would be asked the hard questions. They would stand in the aftermath of misunderstanding or misjudgment.

That knowledge shaped behavior.

It slowed conversations. It encouraged caution. It forced humility.

But in the modern system, the agent often disappears after the sale.

Claims departments take over. Service centers step in. Processes replace presence.

The agent is no longer the final line between promise and consequence.

And while that distance offers relief, it also removes a quiet form of accountability that once anchored the work.

Today, when something goes wrong, the agent is often copied—not contacted. Included—but not needed. Informed—but not responsible.

The call goes to a department. The explanation comes from a policy. The resolution arrives without relationship.

Responsibility dissolves not in conflict, but in silence.

And when you are no longer needed after the sale, it becomes easier—
almost unintentionally—to treat the sale as the finish line instead of
the beginning of responsibility.

That shift is subtle.

But it changes everything.

How the Agent's Role Was Redefined

In earlier eras, the agent was the guardian of the promise. He or she
stood between complexity and consequence. Their judgment mattered
because their presence mattered.

They knew the families. They knew the risks. They knew the cost of
getting it wrong.

In the modern system, the agent increasingly became a conduit.

Products flowed through them. Applications passed across their desk.
Policies were delivered efficiently.

The role shifted from interpreter to distributor.

At first, this felt like relief.

Less emotional burden. Less personal risk. Less responsibility for
outcomes beyond the sale.

But that relief came at a price.

When responsibility thins, vocation fades.

When Selling Replaced Stewardship

Selling is not immoral.

But selling without stewardship is dangerous.

Stewardship requires patience. Selling rewards urgency.

Stewardship requires listening. Selling rewards talking.

Stewardship demands the courage to say no. Selling punishes restraint.

As compensation models leaned harder into volume and growth, the internal tension increased. Agents felt pressure to produce, not to protect. Conversations shortened. Reviews became optional. Explanations turned into summaries.

Not because agents wanted to cut corners—but because the system incentivized speed over depth.

Over time, this changed how the work felt.

The Emotional Cost of Weightlessness

When work loses its weight, something unexpected happens.

It becomes harder to feel proud of it.

Wins feel hollow. Losses feel distant. Burnout arrives quietly.

Many agents experience this without understanding it. They hit goals. They earn incentives. They achieve outward success—yet feel disconnected from the purpose that once drew them to the profession.

This disconnect is often mislabeled as fatigue or lack of motivation.

In reality, it is moral dissonance—the gap between what the work once demanded and what it now rewards.

People are not wired to perform consequential work without consequence.

When everything becomes abstract, meaning erodes.

Why This Matters More Than Ever

This is not a critique of technology or growth.

It is a reminder that progress without conscience always extracts a cost.

Insurance did not lose its weight because agents stopped caring.

It lost its weight because systems made caring optional.

And optional responsibility eventually becomes avoided responsibility.

Chapter 3 exists to bring that weight back into view.

Not to shame. Not to indict. But to ask an honest question:

What kind of professional do you want to be when no one is watching?

Most agents do not wake up one day and decide to abandon their principles.

That is not how moral erosion works.

It happens quietly. Incrementally. Under pressure that feels reasonable in the moment and invisible in hindsight. The pressure does not arrive as force. It arrives as expectation.

Numbers to hit. Activity to show. Momentum to maintain.

At first, these expectations feel normal. Even healthy. Accountability matters. Production matters. Growth matters.

But over time, the pressure begins to ask for something different.

Not dishonesty. Not manipulation. Just compromise.

Small ones. Convenient ones. Easily justified ones.

The First Compromise Is Almost Always Rational

The first compromise almost never feels unethical.

It feels practical.

An agent explains less than they could have. They skip a review they know would have helped. They assume understanding instead of confirming it.

The reasoning is immediate and convincing.

"They just want the price." "We can clean it up later." "Nothing bad is likely to happen."

And most of the time, nothing bad does happen.

The policy issues. The client is satisfied. The system records a win.

So the behavior repeats.

This is how moral injury begins—not with harm, but with unresolved dissonance.

When Quotas Replace Judgment

Quotas are not inherently unethical.

But they are indifferent to nuance.

A quota does not care whether coverage fits the life it insures. It does not care whether understanding is complete. It does not care whether restraint would have been wiser.

It only cares whether the number moves.

Judgment, by contrast, is slow.

Jugement ask questions. Jugement pauses. Judgment sometimes says not yet or not this.

When quotas and judgment collide, something has to give.

Too often, judgment yields quietly—not because the agent disagrees with it, but because the system does not reward it.

The Agent Knows — Even When No One Else Does

This is the part few people talk about.

Agents know when they could have slowed down. They know when a conversation deserved more care. They know when a recommendation was convenient rather than complete.

No one else may ever notice.

The client is satisfied. The policy is issued. The paperwork is correct.

But the agent remembers.

Each compromise leaves a residue—not visible, but felt.

Over time, that residue accumulates.

The Subtle Loss of Trust in Oneself

One of the most damaging consequences of moral injury is internal.

The agent begins to distrust their own instincts.

Not because those instincts are wrong—but because they interfere with momentum.

Listening takes time. Clarifying creates friction. Slowing down threatens production.

So instincts are overridden often enough that they begin to quiet themselves.

This is not burnout.

It is erosion of identity.

The Stories Agents Tell Themselves

To survive this erosion, agents develop stories.

Not lies—stories.

"Everyone does it this way." "The carrier approved it." "If it was really wrong, someone would stop me." "The client didn't ask."

These narratives are not malicious. They are protective. They allow good people to function inside systems that reward speed over depth.

Language becomes armor.

Responsibility is redistributed. Ownership is diluted. Conscience is deferred.

Over time, these stories harden into habit.

Success That Doesn't Sit Right

This is why some of the most financially successful agents feel the most disconnected.

They are winning by the system's standards—but losing by their own.

Bonuses arrive. Recognition follows. Momentum builds.

From the outside, everything looks right.

From the inside, something feels hollow.

The work produces results—but not pride.

This is not exhaustion from long hours.

It is discomfort from misalignment.

Why This Is So Hard to Admit

Admitting moral injury is difficult because it does not look like failure.

There is no collapse. No scandal. No visible consequence.

The agent is producing. The business is growing. The numbers are strong.

Everything appears fine.

And that is precisely why the fracture persists.

How the System Mislabels the Problem

The system has a name for this feeling.

It calls it burnout.

Burnout is treated as a personal deficiency. A motivation issue. A resilience problem.

So the solutions follow predictably.

Time off. New incentives. Fresh goals.

But rest does not heal moral injury.

Incentives do not resolve misalignment.

Burnout is not the disease.

It is the symptom.

What Happens When the Agent Stops Listening to Himself

Eventually, something shifts.

The agent stops arguing internally. The questions soften. The discomfort dulls.

Not because alignment has returned—but because the signal has been muted.

Conversations become efficient but shallow. Recommendations become standard but safe. Language becomes mechanical.

The agent still performs—but no longer feels present.

Clients are handled competently, not carefully. Decisions are justified, not examined. Responsibility is shared, not owned.

This numbness is not relief.

It is retreat.

And once retreat becomes normal, returning to conscience feels risky—almost disruptive.

When Clients Become Categories

As the fracture widens, posture changes.

Conversations become transactional. Clients become segments. Needs become checklists.

Not out of cruelty—but out of self-protection.

Distance dulls discomfort.

If the client is a category, the decision carries less weight. If the conversation is scripted, responsibility feels shared. If the outcome is processed, consequence feels abstract.

This is how good people adapt to systems that quietly ask them to compromise.

What Integrity Costs in a System That Doesn't Reward It

Doing the right thing has a cost—especially in systems that measure success narrowly.

It costs time. It costs momentum. It sometimes costs recognition.

The agent who slows down may miss a number. The agent who asks harder questions may lose a sale. The agent who insists on clarity may appear inefficient.

Over time, this creates loneliness.

Not isolation—but separation.

You begin to realize that integrity is rarely celebrated in real time. It is noticed only in hindsight—often by people who were never in the room when the decision was made.

That is why compromise becomes tempting.

Not because agents are weak—but because they are human.

The Cost of Ignoring the Fracture

Left unaddressed, the fracture deepens.

Cynicism replaces curiosity. Language becomes guarded. Purpose becomes performative.

Eventually, the work becomes something to endure rather than something to honor.

That is the real cost.

Not to the carrier. Not to the agency.

But to the person doing the work.

Why This Chapter Exists

Chapter 3 exists to name what most agents feel but rarely articulate.

The problem is not that agents lack integrity.

The problem is that the system slowly trains them to set it aside—and then calls the result burnout.

Burnout is not weakness.

It is a signal.

And ignoring that signal does not make it disappear.

It only makes it quieter

No one teaches agents how to become someone else.

It happens naturally.

When misalignment lasts long enough, the mind adapts. The conscience does not disappear—it reorganizes. It learns which questions to silence and which explanations to repeat. It learns where resistance creates friction and where compliance creates ease.

This is how a professional mask forms.

Not as deception. Not as performance.

But as protection.

The agent still shows up. Still produces. Still speaks with confidence.

From the outside, nothing appears broken.

But something essential has shifted beneath the surface.

Language Changes Before Behavior Does

The earliest sign of this shift is language.

Words become less precise. Explanations become smoother. Descriptions become safer.

Complexity is softened. Uncertainty is avoided. Responsibility is generalized.

Phrases begin to replace conversations.

"This is standard." "Most people choose this." "That's just how it works."

These phrases are not lies.

They are shields.

They reduce friction. They shorten conversations. They preserve momentum.

They also quietly remove the agent from ownership.

What once required discernment becomes routine. What once demanded care becomes procedural. What once invited dialogue becomes a conclusion delivered with confidence.

The agent does not feel dishonest.

They feel efficient.

When Confidence Replaces Conviction

Confidence is easy to mistake for conviction.

Confidence sounds certain. Conviction carries weight.

Confidence speaks smoothly. Conviction sometimes hesitates.

As the mask forms, confidence becomes the default posture.

It is safer than conviction. Cleaner than honesty. More efficient than reflection.

The agent learns how to speak without revealing doubt. How to guide without inviting scrutiny. How to reassure without fully engaging.

Clients feel comforted. Systems feel satisfied.

But conviction—the internal alignment between belief and action—begins to thin.

And when conviction fades, accountability becomes abstract.

The Professional Persona

Over time, the agent develops a professional persona.

This persona is competent. Measured. Unflappable.

It knows what to say. Knows how to pivot. Knows how to keep conversations moving forward.

The persona performs well.

But it also insulates.

When outcomes disappoint, the persona absorbs the impact. When questions arise, the persona explains them away. When doubt surfaces, the persona redirects.

The real self stays protected behind it.

At first, this separation feels useful.

After all, distance reduces emotional strain. It allows productivity without vulnerability. It keeps work from spilling into the rest of life.

But separation, left unexamined, becomes distance.

The Cost of Always Being "Fine"

One of the most dangerous phrases in professional life is:

"I'm fine."

The agent says it often. Believes it sometimes.

After all, the numbers are good. The clients are stable. The business is functioning.

But "fine" is not neutral.

It is a signal that deeper questions have been postponed.

The agent is no longer asking: Do I believe in this recommendation? Would I make this choice if no one were watching? Does this align with who I want to be?

Those questions feel disruptive. They threaten efficiency. They complicate momentum.

So they are avoided.

How the Mask Changes the Client Relationship

Clients are perceptive.

They may not understand policies, endorsements, or exclusions—but they understand posture. They sense presence. They feel whether a conversation is open or closed.

As the professional mask settles in, the client relationship subtly changes.

Conversations become shorter. Recommendations become firmer. Questions feel less welcome.

Not because the agent intends to shut clients down—but because the mask is designed to keep things moving forward.

The agent speaks with authority. The client nods. Decisions are made efficiently.

But something is missing.

The space for uncertainty disappears.

Clients stop asking why and begin asking only how much. They sense that the explanation is already complete, that the conversation has an endpoint, that probing further would be inconvenient.

Trust becomes procedural.

Not relational. Not earned through depth.

But maintained through smoothness.

The agent notices this shift but rarely names it.

Clients seem satisfied. Complaints are rare. Everything appears to be working.

Yet the relationship has changed.

The agent is no longer with the client in the decision. The agent is leading the client through it.

This feels professional. It feels competent.

But it also creates distance.

Over time, clients stop seeing the agent as a guide and start seeing them as a provider. The relationship becomes transactional—even when the tone remains friendly.

And transactions require less conscience than relationships do.

The Moment an Agent Realizes They're Performing

There is a moment—often quiet—when the agent realizes something has shifted.

It does not arrive during a sale. Or a review. Or a moment of conflict.

It arrives in stillness.

The agent hears themselves speak and thinks:

"I've said this exact sentence a hundred times." "This sounds polished—but it doesn't feel personal." "I'm delivering something, not discussing it."

The realization is unsettling.

Because the performance is effective.

Clients respond well. The system approves. The numbers move.

And yet, the agent feels strangely absent from their own words.

Language has become rehearsed. Explanations feel scripted. Confidence no longer requires conviction.

The work begins to resemble theater.

Not dishonesty—performance.

The agent knows how to play the role. Knows when to pause. Knows when to reassure. Knows when to close.

But the role has begun to replace the self.

This is not burnout.

It is dissonance.

And once an agent notices this, it becomes difficult to unsee.

The question is no longer "Am I good at this?"

It becomes:

"Who am I becoming by doing it this way?"

The Subtle Trade Being Made

Without realizing it, the agent makes a quiet trade.

Depth for efficiency. Presence for productivity. Conviction for confidence.

Nothing is lost all at once.

But something meaningful is surrendered over time.

The agent becomes very good at the role—and less connected to the reason they entered it.

The Question That Refuses to Disappear

Despite the mask, one question never fully leaves:

"Is this who I wanted to become?"

It does not accuse. It does not demand.

It waits.

Waiting is its power.

The question surfaces not in crisis, but in clarity—when the agent finally pauses long enough to hear it.

Weight does not return on its own.

It does not drift back with time. It does not reappear because the market improves. It does not arrive with a new title, a better system, or a larger book of business.

Weight must be chosen.

Not loudly. Not publicly. Not for recognition.

But deliberately.

The moment an agent realizes the work has become weightless is not a failure. It is a reckoning. A quiet moment of clarity where the professional finally sees the distance between what they do and what they meant to do.

That moment is uncomfortable.

Most people rush past it.

They distract themselves with activity. They bury it in numbers. They tell themselves the feeling will pass.

But those who don't rush—those who pause—are given a choice.

To continue drifting. Or to re-anchor.

Responsibility Is Not Assigned — It Is Assumed

Responsibility is not something the system hands you.

It cannot be mandated by compliance. It cannot be enforced by compensation. It cannot be automated by process.

Responsibility is assumed.

A professional chooses to carry responsibility even when no one requires it. Even when the system allows them to set it down. Even when no penalty exists for avoiding it.

They choose to slow conversations when speed is rewarded. They choose to explain what is inconvenient. They choose to ask questions that may cost them a sale.

This choice rarely announces itself.

It happens quietly.

In a moment where an easier explanation would suffice. In a conversation where silence would allow a quick close. In a decision where "good enough" would pass unnoticed.

That is where weight returns.

Not in grand gestures—but in restraint.

Weight Requires Presence — And Presence Is Costly

You cannot carry weight at a distance.

Distance is how responsibility dissolves.

Weight requires presence.

Presence means staying in the conversation longer than is comfortable. It means allowing uncertainty to surface instead of smoothing it over. It means resisting the urge to rescue the moment with confidence when what it actually needs is patience.

Presence makes decisions heavier.

That is not a flaw.

That is the point.

A professional who carries weight does not rush to resolution. They sit with the implications. They recognize that every recommendation touches a real life, not an abstract risk.

Presence demands emotional availability.

And emotional availability always costs something.

It costs energy. It costs efficiency. It costs emotional safety.

But it gives something back that systems cannot provide.

Meaning.

The Courage to Reclaim Conviction

Conviction is not bravado.

It is not certainty delivered loudly. It is not confidence practiced until it sounds rehearsed.

Conviction is alignment.

It is the quiet agreement between what you believe and what you recommend. It is the willingness to stand behind a decision even when it slows you down. Even when it isolates you. Even when no one applauds.

Conviction requires courage because it often feels lonely.

The professional who carries weight may look inefficient. They may appear overly cautious. They may be misunderstood by peers who optimize for speed.

But they sleep better.

Because conviction steadies the work from the inside.

When conviction returns, explanations sound like truth instead of delivery. Decisions feel owned instead of defended. The work stops feeling performative.

It becomes whole again.

Redefining Success — Quietly

When weight returns, success changes definition.

Not publicly. Privately.

Success is no longer speed. It is suitability.

Success is no longer volume. It is fit.

Success is no longer approval. It is integrity.

These metrics do not appear on dashboards. They are not celebrated in meetings. They do not come with plaques or bonuses.

They appear in conscience.

They show up in how the work feels at the end of the day. In whether you recognize yourself in your own decisions. In whether your explanations still sound like you.

This form of success is quieter.

And far more durable.

The Cost — And the Quiet Reward

Carrying weight costs something.

It costs time. It costs convenience. It sometimes costs opportunity.

You may lose sales you could have closed. You may move slower than peers around you. You may feel out of step with the pace the industry celebrates.

But weight gives something back.

Pride. Clarity. Peace.

The work begins to feel solid again. Grounded. Worth doing.

The internal friction eases—not because the work is easier, but because it is aligned.

Alignment does not remove difficulty.

It removes doubt.

The First Time You Choose Weight Again

The return of weight is rarely dramatic.

It does not arrive with applause or affirmation. It does not announce itself as a turning point.

It usually shows up in a small, almost forgettable moment.

A client asks a question that would be easier to answer simply. A recommendation could be made quickly, confidently, and without friction. The path forward is obvious—and convenient.

And for a moment, the old instinct appears.

Move it along. Close it out. Say what works.

Then something interrupts that reflex.

A pause.

The agent slows down.

They ask one more question. They explain one more implication. They acknowledge uncertainty instead of smoothing it over.

The room gets quieter.

The conversation takes longer.

The outcome becomes less predictable.

This is what choosing weight looks like in practice.

It feels inefficient. It feels exposed. It feels risky.

But it also feels honest.

That first choice is rarely perfect.

The explanation may be clumsy. The silence may feel awkward. The result may even cost the sale.

But something shifts internally.

For the first time in a long while, the agent feels present.

Not performing. Not delivering. Not managing perception.

Present.

And once that happens, it becomes difficult to return to weightlessness.

The agent realizes something important:

The work feels heavier—but it also feels truer.

That moment becomes a reference point.

A quiet reminder that responsibility is not theoretical. It is practiced. It is chosen again and again, in small moments that never make it onto a report.

Weight returns the same way it was lost.

Gradually. Quietly. Through habit.

Why This Choice Matters Beyond You

Weight does not stay contained.

When one professional chooses to carry it, the environment changes.

Clients feel the difference. They sense care instead of performance. They feel guided rather than processed.

Colleagues notice it. Not because it is announced—but because tone shifts. Conversations slow. Language changes.

Culture moves quietly.

Weight is contagious.

Not because it spreads loudly—but because it reminds others of what the work can be.

The Invitation That Remains

This chapter does not demand change.

It offers it.

You can continue performing. Or you can return to practicing.

You can optimize for efficiency. Or you can choose responsibility.

The difference will not be obvious to the system.

But it will be unmistakable to you.

Because when weight returns, the work stops feeling hollow.

And for a profession built on promises, that matters.

"Character is much easier kept than recovered.

Thomas Paine

Chapter 4: The Rise of the Transaction

There was a time when insurance was unmistakably personal.

Not because the products were simpler—though they often were—but because the work required proximity. Agents knew the people they served. They knew their homes, their businesses, their families, and often their struggles. They recognized voices before policy numbers. They remembered names without looking them up.

Insurance lived close to real life.

Decisions were not abstract. Consequences were not theoretical. When coverage failed, the agent did not hear about it through a report or a dashboard—they heard about it at the kitchen table, in church pews, or on the sidewalk outside a closed storefront.

And when they heard it, they did not leave quickly.

They stayed. They listened. They absorbed the silence that followed bad news.

That proximity shaped behavior.

It forced care. It demanded accountability. It made shortcuts expensive. Because shortcuts had faces. And faces had names. And names did not disappear when the meeting ended.

When insurance was personal, responsibility was unavoidable.

When the Outcome Had a Face

In those earlier days, advice lingered.

An agent didn't just make a recommendation and move on. They carried it with them—sometimes for years—because they would likely face the outcome. They would see the family again. They would walk past the business they insured. They would hear about the claim long after the paperwork was finished.

That knowledge changed how advice was given.

It slowed conversations. It sharpened judgment. It made certainty feel dangerous and humility feel necessary.

When you know you will have to stand in front of someone after the outcome, you speak differently. You soften your confidence. You choose honesty over speed. You leave space for uncertainty, because uncertainty is safer than false assurance.

The work had weight because the relationship did.

And weight changes how a person carries themselves.

The Role of the Agent Was Once Clear

The agent was not a distributor.

They were a custodian of risk. A translator of complexity. A steady presence in moments people hoped would never arrive.

They did not simply sell protection—they stood with people when protection was tested.

The work moved at the pace of conversation, not dashboards.

Policies were explained because they had to be understood. Coverage decisions were revisited because lives changed. Recommendations carried weight because the agent would be there if they failed.

The profession assumed continuity.

You would still be there tomorrow. You would still answer the phone. You would still face the outcome of today's advice.

That expectation anchored behavior.

It created a quiet discipline.

You did not rush advice you would have to defend later. You did not simplify decisions you would have to explain again. You did not disappear when the work became uncomfortable.

What Changed Wasn't Intent — It Was Distance

The shift did not begin with bad motives.

It began with distance.

As markets expanded and systems scaled, insurance moved farther away from the places it once lived. Decisions that were once made face-to-face began happening across screens. Relationships stretched thinner. Time compressed.

Efficiency became the goal.

Not because efficiency is wrong—but because it is measurable.

Judgment is not.

Distance softened consequence.

You could give advice and never see the result. You could close a policy and move on. You could meet your numbers without witnessing the outcome.

At first, this felt like progress.

Less discomfort. Less emotional weight. Less personal risk.

Nothing felt immediately wrong.

That's how the change took hold.

When Scale Entered the Picture

Scale promised consistency.

Standardization reduced variability. Scripts reduced uncertainty. Processes reduced dependence on individual discretion.

From a systems perspective, this made sense.

But scale introduced something subtle and dangerous:

Detachment.

When decisions could be made without seeing the person affected by them, the work became lighter. Not easier—lighter.

The emotional gravity faded.

What was once a shared burden became a transaction.

And transactions do not linger.

The Beginning of the Transactional Mindset

As distance increased, the work changed shape.

Insurance began to resemble commerce more than stewardship.

Clients became accounts. Coverage became a bundle. Advice became a recommendation optimized for conversion.

This was not corruption.

It was adaptation.

But adaptation always carries a cost.

The further insurance moved from relationship, the easier it became to treat outcomes as numbers instead of experiences. Loss became an event, not a moment. Claims became files, not conversations.

The work continued.

But it no longer stayed with you.

When Personal Knowledge Became Inefficient

Personal knowledge takes time.

It requires listening. It requires memory. It requires context.

As speed became the metric, personal knowledge became a liability.

Knowing too much slowed decisions. Asking too many questions disrupted flow. Explaining too thoroughly created friction.

So the work simplified.

Not in substance—but in engagement.

Agents still cared.

But caring quietly shifted from involvement to intention.

And intention, without proximity, fades.

The Subtle Loss of Accountability

When insurance stopped being personal, accountability didn't disappear.

It dispersed.

Responsibility became shared. Abstracted. Delayed.

You could make a recommendation and never see the result. You could succeed without knowing whether the advice truly fit. You could perform well and still feel strangely disconnected.

The work kept moving.

But something essential had been lost.

And the loss was quiet enough that most people never named it.

A Quiet Question for the Reader

There's a moment many professionals recognize—though they rarely speak about it.

It's the realization that a client's situation no longer stays with you after the meeting ends.

You do the work well. You follow the process. You meet expectations.

But the human weight fades quickly.

You don't think about the decision later that evening. You don't wonder how it plays out. You don't feel pulled back into it.

That is not failure.

It is distance.

And distance changes everything.

Why This Matters

This chapter is not nostalgia.

It is context.

Understanding how insurance became transactional explains why so many professionals feel disconnected today—even when they are successful.

It explains why the work feels lighter. Why decisions feel reversible. Why conviction feels optional.

And it sets the stage for the next part of the chapter, where we examine what replaced judgment—and what that replacement quietly cost the profession.

Judgment is difficult to measure.

It lives in conversation. It reveals itself over time. It often resists certainty.

Judgment asks questions that do not resolve cleanly. It lingers. It complicates. It forces a professional to sit with uncertainty longer than is comfortable.

Metrics, on the other hand, are obedient.

They are clean. They are immediate. They produce answers without requiring interpretation.

When a profession grows large enough, metrics inevitably arrive—not because judgment is wrong, but because judgment is inconvenient.

Insurance was no exception.

The Appeal of Measurement

Measurement promised clarity.

Numbers removed ambiguity. Dashboards replaced memory. Targets replaced discretion.

For organizations tasked with scale, this was not malicious—it was practical.

Judgment varies. People differ. Context complicates.

Metrics simplify.

They make performance visible. They allow comparison. They reward consistency.

And slowly, almost imperceptibly, what could be measured began to matter more than what could be understood.

Not because understanding was dismissed—but because it could not be displayed.

When Judgment Became Subjective

Judgment is personal.

It requires experience. It depends on context. It cannot be applied uniformly without distortion.

As systems grew, judgment became harder to defend.

One agent's caution looked like another's inefficiency. One professional's restraint looked like another's hesitation. One person's integrity looked like another's missed opportunity.

Judgment required explanation.

Metrics did not.

Metrics solved this tension by removing interpretation.

They did not ask why. They only asked how many.

The Shift in What Was Rewarded

Once metrics entered the room, behavior followed.

Speed was rewarded. Volume was rewarded. Consistency was rewarded.

Care was not punished—but it was no longer visible.

An agent who slowed down to explain nuance did not appear on a leaderboard. A professional who declined a sale did not register in performance reports. A judgment call that prevented future harm did not show up anywhere at all.

What could not be counted slowly lost influence.

And what lost influence slowly lost practice.

When the Work Learned to Perform

Metrics do not create bad behavior.

They shape incentives.

And incentives shape attention.

Agents learned—often unconsciously—where to focus.

They learned which conversations mattered. Which questions slowed progress. Which explanations created friction.

They learned to move efficiently.

Not dishonestly. Not recklessly.

Efficiently.

Efficiency became a survival skill.

And survival skills, once learned, become habits.

The Quiet Redefinition of "Good"

As measurement took hold, the definition of good shifted.

Good became productive. Good became consistent. Good became repeatable.

Judgment did not disappear—but it was quietly reframed.

It became secondary. Optional. Something applied only when time allowed.

The work still functioned.

But it no longer asked the same questions.

And professionals noticed—though they often couldn't articulate what felt different.

When Numbers Began to Feel Safer

Judgment carries risk.

If a judgment call fails, it belongs to the person who made it.

Metrics distribute responsibility.

If the numbers are met, the decision is defensible—even if the outcome is imperfect.

This felt safer.

Following the system provided cover. Hitting the target reduced exposure. Meeting expectations softened accountability.

No one had to say it aloud.

The relief was internal.

The Emotional Relief — And the Trade

For many professionals, metrics brought relief.

No more ambiguity. No more second-guessing. No more lingering uncertainty.

Just targets. Just progress. Just movement.

Days became easier to explain.

But relief always comes with a trade.

What metrics removed in uncertainty, they also removed in weight.

Judgment had once required presence. Metrics allowed distance.

And distance, once introduced, does not reverse easily.

The Slow Displacement of Professional Instinct

Over time, professionals adjusted.

They still had instincts—but they trusted them less. They still sensed misalignment—but they deferred. They still felt hesitation—but they moved anyway.

They told themselves they would revisit it later. That there would be time. That this was just how the work was done now.

The system rewarded momentum.

And momentum rarely pauses for reflection.

Judgment became something you exercised after the numbers were met—if there was time.

Why This Wasn't Obvious at First

This shift did not feel like loss.

It felt like modernization.

The work looked cleaner. The language sounded more professional. The process appeared more controlled.

Outcomes were easier to track—even if they were harder to feel.

And because nothing immediately broke, the change went largely unquestioned.

The Cost That Took Time to Appear

The cost of replacing judgment with metrics was not immediate.

It emerged slowly.

In conversations that felt rushed. In decisions that felt reversible. In work that no longer lingered after it was done.

Professionals became efficient—but less anchored.

Successful—but less certain.

They completed days without feeling connected to the outcome of their work.

And that absence—quiet, unremarkable at first—was the real cost.

What Was Quietly Exchanged

What was exchanged was not competence.

The profession did not become careless. It did not forget how to work. It did not abandon effort.

It exchanged judgment for insulation.

Metrics made decisions easier to justify. They made outcomes easier to explain. They made responsibility easier to distribute.

And in doing so, they changed what it felt like to be responsible.

The work no longer asked professionals to stand alone with their decisions. It asked them to stand inside the system.

That distinction mattered more than anyone realized at the time.

Because standing alone requires conviction. Standing inside a system requires compliance.

Over time, professionals adjusted their posture.

They leaned less on instinct. They deferred more often to process. They trusted numbers because numbers did not ask anything of them emotionally.

This was not a collapse.

It was a trade.

The work became lighter to carry— but also easier to set down.

And once responsibility becomes something that can be set down, it rarely feels the same when picked back up.

Speed does not announce itself as a problem.

It arrives as improvement.

Faster responses feel like better service. Shorter cycles feel like efficiency. Higher throughput feels like growth.

In isolation, none of this is wrong.

But when speed becomes the primary measure of progress, the work begins to change shape—quietly, subtly, and often without protest.

When Faster Started to Feel Smarter

Speed simplifies decision-making.

It narrows options. It compresses conversation. It rewards decisiveness over deliberation.

In fast environments, hesitation begins to look like incompetence. Reflection looks like delay. Silence looks like uncertainty—and uncertainty feels unsafe.

And so the work learns to move.

Not recklessly. Not irresponsibly.

Quickly.

Speed becomes a proxy for confidence, even when confidence has not been earned. The ability to respond immediately is mistaken for understanding. Momentum is mistaken for mastery.

Over time, the professional stops asking whether speed serves the work—and begins assuming that it does.

Scale Didn't Just Increase Volume — It Changed Behavior

Scale did not simply allow more people to be served.

It changed what behavior was rewarded.

As organizations grew, systems were designed to handle more, not to pause longer. Processes were built for flow, not reflection. Anything that slowed movement was treated as friction—something to be engineered out.

Judgment introduced friction. Conversation introduced delay. Context introduced variability.

Speed solved all three.

And in solving them, it quietly displaced the very elements that once gave the work its gravity.

The Comfort of Momentum

Momentum is comforting.

When things are moving, they feel alive. When numbers rise, they feel validated. When queues clear quickly, they feel controlled.

Momentum reassures professionals that they are doing something right—even when they are unsure what that something is.

In fast systems, stopping feels dangerous.

To slow down is to risk falling behind. To question is to interrupt flow. To hesitate is to draw attention to oneself.

And so the work keeps moving.

Not because movement is always right— but because stillness feels risky.

When Urgency Replaced Importance

Speed changes what rises to the surface.

Urgent matters rise. Important ones wait.

Simple decisions get resolved. Complex ones are deferred. Conversations that conclude quickly are favored over those that require patience.

Nothing is explicitly abandoned. Nothing is declared unimportant.

It is simply postponed—again and again—until postponement becomes habit.

Over time, the work begins to favor what can be completed over what should be considered.

The Shrinking Space for Judgment

Judgment needs space.

It needs time to surface unease. It needs room for doubt. It needs permission to be unfinished.

Speed compresses that space.

Decisions are made with less information. Recommendations are delivered with fewer qualifiers. Outcomes are accepted before they are fully understood.

Judgment does not disappear—but it is rushed.

And rushed judgment rarely feels like judgment at all. It feels like compliance wearing the mask of decisiveness.

The Illusion of Progress

Speed produces output.

Scale multiplies it.

Together, they create activity that looks like advancement.

More policies written. More interactions completed. More metrics achieved.

The system appears healthy.

But activity is not the same as progress.

Progress implies direction. Activity only implies motion.

When speed and scale dominate, direction is assumed rather than examined. The work moves forward without regularly asking toward what.

Where Responsibility Began to Slip

In fast systems, responsibility becomes transient.

A decision is made, handed off, and absorbed by the next process. Accountability moves—but it does not linger. No one stays with the outcome long enough to feel its weight.

The faster the system moves, the easier it is for responsibility to fall between steps.

Not because anyone intends it to—but because no one is positioned to hold it.

Responsibility becomes something passed forward rather than carried.

The Emotional Cost to the Profession

This is where the loss became personal—though few recognized it at the time.

Professionals remained busy, productive, and successful. But something in the work began to feel thin.

Days ended without reflection. Decisions concluded without resonance. Outcomes felt provisional—replaceable.

The work no longer stayed with people after it was done.

There was satisfaction in completion, but less fulfillment in consequence. Pride became quieter. Conviction felt less necessary.

The profession did not lose competence.

It lost connection.

When the Work Stopped Touching Back

In earlier eras, the work pushed back.

It lingered. It followed professionals home. It demanded emotional presence.

Speed and scale softened that friction.

The work ended when the task ended, not when the impact was understood. Closure was procedural, not human.

And over time, the profession grew accustomed to that distance.

Not because it preferred it—but because it was efficient.

Why This Felt Like Advancement

Speed and scale arrived alongside technology, data, and access.

They felt modern. They felt inevitable. They felt necessary.

Questioning them felt regressive.

To slow down felt like resistance. To insist on deliberation felt outdated. To ask for patience felt impractical.

And so the profession adapted—quickly.

But adaptation always reshapes the thing adapting.

What Was Quietly Lost Along the Way

What was lost was not effort.

People worked harder. They stayed longer. They produced more.

What was lost was orientation.

The work stopped asking professionals to locate themselves inside the consequence of their decisions. It moved quickly enough that reflection became optional—and optional things rarely survive long.

Responsibility became mobile.

And once responsibility becomes mobile, it becomes lighter.

The Weight the Profession No Longer Felt

This loss did not announce itself as grief.

It showed up as restlessness. As detachment. As a vague sense that something meaningful had thinned.

The industry gained efficiency—but lost intimacy. It gained reach—but lost resonance.

The work continued.

But it no longer pressed back in the same way.

Where This Leaves the Profession

Speed and scale did not break insurance.

But they stretched it.

They thinned the moments where judgment once lived. They narrowed the spaces where responsibility could settle.

And they left behind a profession that moves quickly—often impressively—but struggles to slow itself when slowing matters most.

The profession did not lose its skill.

It lost its center.

Insurance did not become incapable. It became distracted.

Distracted by speed. Distracted by scale. Distracted by measurement.

And in that distraction, something essential was left unguarded.

What was left unguarded was not procedure.

It was presence.

Presence is the willingness to remain near the consequence of your words.

It is the discipline to stay when it would be easier to leave. It is the courage to sit in uncertainty when resolution is not yet available. It is the humility to admit what cannot be promised.

Presence cannot be standardized. It cannot be automated. It cannot be optimized without losing itself.

And because it cannot be measured, it was never fully protected.

The systems that grew around the profession did not account for it. The incentives that shaped behavior did not reward it. The metrics that guided performance did not require it.

And so presence became optional.

And optional things rarely survive.

When Responsibility Became Abstract

Responsibility once had a face.

It was the person sitting across the table. It was the family whose future depended on a decision. It was the business whose survival rested on advice.

The work pressed back.

It asked the professional to feel the weight of consequence before moving forward.

As the work became transactional, responsibility became conceptual.

Outcomes became numbers. Losses became data. Protection became a product.

The human consequence receded.

And when consequence recedes, so does restraint.

Not because restraint is no longer valued—but because it is no longer demanded.

The Cost We Never Calculated

The industry calculated risk.

It calculated premium. It calculated exposure. It calculated loss ratios.

But it did not calculate moral cost.

The cost of decisions made without presence. The cost of speed without reflection. The cost of volume without judgment.

These costs do not appear on reports.

They appear in culture.

They appear in how people speak. They appear in how people decide. They appear in how quickly the work is set down.

What Culture Quietly Taught

Culture teaches without instruction.

It teaches what is safe. It teaches what is rewarded. It teaches what is tolerated.

And the culture that formed around transaction taught the profession that:

Speed matters more than understanding. Completion matters more than consequence. Compliance matters more than conviction.

Not because anyone intended it.

But because nothing resisted it.

Over time, the profession learned to move quickly and feel lightly.

The Erosion of Stewardship

Stewardship requires ownership.

It asks the professional to carry the outcome. To remain connected after the transaction ends. To accept responsibility beyond the metric.

Transaction asks only for completion.

.

And over time, completion replaced care.

Not in language. But in behavior.

The work became easier to finish—and harder to honor.

What Stewardship Actually Feels Like

Stewardship is not efficient.

It lingers.

It stays in the room when the conversation is uncomfortable. It returns the call when the answer is uncertain. It revisits the decision when doubt remains.

It feels heavier.

Not because it is wrong—but because it is real.

Stewardship requires the professional to be willing to be affected by their work.

To allow it to touch back.

To let the outcome matter personally, not just procedurally.

This is the weight the profession once carried naturally.

This is the weight that has slowly been set down.

There is a moment every professional recognizes, though few name.

It is the moment when the easy path presents itself.

The recommendation that will close quickly. The solution that will satisfy the metric. The answer that will move the file forward.

And there is, beside it, the heavier path.

The conversation that will take longer. The explanation that may create resistance. The counsel that may cost the sale.

Stewardship lives in this space.

It is not heroic. It is not dramatic. It is quiet.

It is the decision to say, "This may not be what you want to hear, but it is what you need to consider."

It is the willingness to absorb the discomfort that follows.

The pause in the room. The tension in the voice. The uncertainty in the eyes across the table.

These are not inefficiencies.

They are the labor of care.

And they are rarely visible.

There is also a loneliness to this work when it is done well.

Metrics will not praise it. Dashboards will not record it. Reports will not reward it.

Often, no one will know it occurred.

The professional will leave the room with nothing to show but the quiet knowledge that the right thing was done.

This is a heavy thing to carry.

And it is precisely this weight that the profession has slowly learned to avoid.

Over time, the work offers alternatives.

"Just move it forward." "Don't complicate it." "Let the system handle it."

These phrases are not cruel.

They are comfortable.

They promise relief.

They offer distance.

They remove the necessity of standing alone with a decision.

And each time they are accepted, the work becomes easier—and thinner.

What is lost in this thinning is not performance.

It is meaning.

A profession sustained only by efficiency will eventually exhaust its people.

Not from labor—but from emptiness.

When the work no longer presses back, it no longer teaches.

When the work no longer teaches, it no longer forms professionals— only operators.

And operators do not inherit a calling.

They inherit a function.

The long cost is cultural.

New professionals enter a system where the weight is no longer modeled.

They learn speed before judgment. They learn output before ownership. They learn completion before consequence.

Not because they are careless.

But because this is what they see.

And culture is the loudest teacher.

To choose stewardship today is to swim against a current.

It is to accept that the work will sometimes be slower, harder, and lonelier.

It is to believe that responsibility is not a burden to be minimized, but a trust to be honored.

And it is to understand that the weight of the work is not the problem.

The absence of that weight is.

The Interior Cost to the Professional

There is a quiet cost when the work no longer presses back.

The days become smoother—but less meaningful. The decisions become easier—but less anchored. The success becomes measurable—but less satisfying.

The professional becomes efficient.

But also distant.

And distance, over time, dulls conviction.

What once felt like calling begins to feel like function.

And function alone does not sustain a profession.

What Must Be Remembered

The profession does not need to be saved.

It needs to be remembered.

Remembered not as a sales function, but as a human one.
Remembered not as a product business, but as a stewardship calling.
Remembered not as distribution, but as responsibility.

Insurance was never meant to be light.

It was meant to be carried.

The Return Is Not Backward

This is not a call to abandon progress.

It is a call to anchor it.

Speed must be guided by judgment. Scale must be governed by care. Measurement must be tempered by presence.

Without these, progress becomes motion without meaning.

The Profession's Quiet Choice

Every generation inherits a version of this work.

And every generation decides what to protect.

Not through policy. But through practice.

The profession now faces a quiet choice:

To remain efficient. Or to become responsible again.

To be fast. Or to be faithful to the weight of the work.

To complete transactions. Or to carry consequences.

Closing Reflection

Insurance is not merely about transferring risk.

It is about holding it.

And what is held carefully is rarely treated lightly.

The transaction will always exist.

But it must never become the point.

"You don't build a business — you build people, and then people build the Business."

Zig Ziglar

CHAPTER 5: The Steward's Way

Stewardship is not a technique.

It is not a script. It is not a strategy.

It is a posture.

It is how a professional chooses to stand in relation to another person's risk.

Before there were systems, before there were policies, before there were dashboards and metrics, there was simply a man or woman sitting across from another, listening.

And deciding whether the work would be light—or whether it would be carried.

Stewardship begins in that moment.

Not when a product is selected. Not when a quote is delivered. But when the professional decides how seriously to take what has been entrusted.

The Return to Weight

A steward does not rush the important.

They understand that speed is sometimes necessary—but never sovereign.

They know that efficiency is valuable—but not ultimate.

They recognize that clarity is earned, not extracted.

Stewardship is the refusal to treat another person's future as a transaction.

It is the discipline of presence in a world that rewards absence.

It is the willingness to stay when it would be easier to move on.

A Quiet Room, A Real Decision

There is a moment in every professional's career when stewardship stops being an idea and becomes a choice.

The room is quiet. The file is open. The recommendation is clear.

And yet something inside resists.

Not because the answer is wrong, but because it is incomplete.

This is the moment when the steward feels the weight.

The easy solution is available. The faster answer is ready. The transaction could be completed.

And still, the steward pauses.

Not to delay.

But to consider what will remain after the conversation ends.

What It Means to Carry

To carry responsibility is to accept that your words will echo beyond the room.

It is to speak with awareness that reassurance, too easily given, can become regret.

It is to choose honesty over harmony.

Not because honesty is harsh—but because it is faithful.

The steward understands that comfort is not the same as care.

Sometimes care unsettles.

Sometimes it slows the conversation.

Sometimes it costs the sale.

But it preserves the relationship between the professional and their conscience.

The Dignity of Slow Work

Stewardship dignifies the pace of the work.

It allows time for reflection. It permits uncertainty. It respects the gravity of consequence.

Slow does not mean inefficient.

It means intentional.

It means the work is being done with awareness, not haste.

The steward measures success not only by completion, but by consequence.

Not only by output, but by outcome.

Not only by growth, but by health.

The Quiet Authority of Care

Authority in this profession was never meant to come from volume.

It comes from care.

From consistency. From memory. From faithfulness over time.

Clients do not trust systems.

They trust stewards.

They trust the person who remembers their story. Who anticipates their questions. Who carries their concern as more than a file.

Trust, once earned, is not hurried.

The Loneliness of Integrity

There is a solitude that comes with stewardship.

It is the solitude of standing alone when the easier path is visible.

It is the solitude of explaining what others might simplify.

It is the solitude of carrying responsibility without applause.

The steward is often unseen.

Metrics will not praise this work. Dashboards will not record it. Reports will not reward it.

And yet, this unseen labor is what keeps the profession honest.

The Emotional Cost of Carrying

There is weight in this way of working.

It is not always comfortable.

It is not always efficient.

And it is rarely celebrated.

The steward often leaves the room with less to show, but more to hold.

They carry the uncertainty of their counsel. They carry the quiet hope that their advice was sound. They carry the knowledge that the outcome may not be visible for years.

This is not light work.

But it is meaningful work.

And meaning, not momentum, is what sustains a profession over time.

Why Stewardship Feels Different

Stewardship asks the professional to be affected by the work.

To let it touch back.

To feel the consequence of their decisions, not just their completion.

It resists the illusion that distance is protection.

It understands that detachment is not neutrality—it is absence.

The steward does not hide behind process.

They stand inside responsibility.

Courage to Stand Alone

There will be moments when stewardship feels lonely.

When the easier path is visible.

When the faster answer is available.

When the system would prefer movement over meaning.

In these moments, the steward chooses weight.

They choose to slow.

They choose to explain.

They choose to risk misunderstanding in order to preserve integrity.

This is not heroism.

It is fidelity.

The Restoration of Identity

Stewardship restores something the profession has quietly lost.

It restores dignity.

It allows the professional to see themselves not as a distributor of products, but as a guardian of consequence.

Not as a producer of volume, but as a carrier of trust.

Not as a function, but as a calling.

And a calling, once remembered, reshapes the work.

The Beginning of Renewal

This chapter is not about techniques.

It is about orientation.

It is about remembering how to stand again inside the weight of the work.

It is about returning to a way of practice that does not exhaust the professional, because it does not require them to abandon themselves.

Stewardship is not nostalgia.

It is renewal.

It is the decision to let the work matter again.

There is a kind of good that never announces itself.

It does not arrive with applause. It does not produce immediate reward. It does not generate recognition.

It accumulates quietly.

A careful recommendation given today prevents a loss years from now. A difficult conversation held now spares regret later. A moment of patience preserves a family's stability long after the file is closed.

The steward rarely sees these outcomes.

But they exist.

They compound.

This is the long view of the work.

And it is this long view that separates a profession from a trade.

Stewardship is legacy in motion.

It is the understanding that the work done well today becomes the standard someone else will inherit tomorrow.

The steward plants trees they may never sit beneath.

They build trust they may never personally benefit from.

They protect futures they may never witness.

And yet, this unseen labor is the true architecture of the profession.

There will be seasons when the steward feels behind.

Behind the numbers. Behind the pace. Behind the visible markers of success.

And in those seasons, doubt will whisper that care is inefficient.

But efficiency is not the same as health.

Growth is not the same as durability.

Momentum is not the same as meaning.

The steward learns to measure success by what remains, not only by what moves.

In time, this way of work does something rare.

It allows the professional to look back without regret.

To see a body of work not only as transactions completed, but as trust honored.

Not only as revenue earned, but as responsibility carried.

Not only as effort expended, but as consequence stewarded.

This is the quiet reward of the calling.

Stewardship, in the end, is not about being better than others.

It is about being faithful to the weight of the work.

And faithfulness, practiced long enough, becomes legacy.

Listening is not passive.

It is not silence. It is not waiting for a turn to speak.

It is labor.

It is the discipline of setting aside the need to perform in order to understand.

The steward listens not to respond, but to receive.

And in receiving, the work begins.

There is a difference between hearing and listening, and the difference is weight.

Hearing is mechanical. Listening is intentional.

Hearing processes sound. Listening receives meaning.

The steward does not merely register words. They attend to consequence.

Before there were forms, there were stories.

Before there were policies, there were lives.

The steward understands that no document ever tells the full truth.

Only people do.

And people rarely tell it all at once.

They circle it. They approach it. They test the safety of the room before they reveal what matters.

Listening creates that safety.

True listening requires patience.

It allows pauses. It tolerates repetition. It respects hesitation.

Often, what matters most is spoken slowly, indirectly, and with restraint.

The steward does not rush these moments.

They know that clarity is not extracted—it is revealed.

And revelation cannot be hurried.

There are conversations that seem finished long before they are.

The file appears complete. The need appears defined. The solution appears obvious.

And yet, something inside the steward resists closure.

So they remain.

They ask again. They wait. They listen beyond the surface.

And in that waiting, a different truth often emerges.

A fear not yet named. A risk not yet understood. A consequence not yet considered.

Listening, in these moments, does not save time.

It saves futures.

When a person feels heard, they speak differently.

They speak with less defense. They speak with more honesty. They speak with greater courage.

The steward listens for what is said.

But more importantly, they listen for what is not.

For the hesitation behind the confidence. For the fear beneath the logic. For the story beneath the facts.

Listening is not about gathering information.

It is about recognizing meaning.

Silence is not empty.

It is often full.

It holds reflection. It holds decision. It holds recognition.

The steward is not afraid of this silence.

They know that rushing to fill it often replaces understanding with noise.

And noise rarely protects anyone.

To listen is to accept responsibility for what is heard.

The steward does not collect information.

They receive trust.

And trust, once received, demands care.

Care in how questions are asked. Care in how conclusions are formed. Care in how recommendations are offered.

Listening binds the professional to the outcome.

Many harms in this profession are not caused by malice.

They are caused by speed.

By assumption.

By the pressure to conclude before understanding has finished forming.

Listening resists this harm.

It is a form of protection that feels invisible, but proves powerful.

Over time, the steward learns that listening is not a phase of the process.

It is the process.

Everything else rests upon it.

Advice given without listening is instruction.

Advice given after listening is counsel.

Instruction informs.

Counsel protects.

And protection is the point.

There is a personal cost to this discipline.

To listen deeply is to absorb concern.

To carry stories.

To feel responsibility.

The steward often leaves the room carrying more than they arrived with.

And yet, this burden is also what makes the work honorable.

Trust is not built in transactions.

It is built in attention.

In the willingness to remember. In the discipline to follow up. In the care to remain available long after the sale.

The steward understands that trust compounds slowly, but endures deeply.

A profession that forgets how to listen eventually forgets who it serves.

It begins to solve problems no one actually has. It begins to sell solutions no one truly needs. It begins to optimize processes while neglecting people.

The steward resists this drift.

They return, again and again, to the simple, demanding work of attention.

Most people do not need to be convinced.

They need to be understood.

Listening offers this gift.

And a gift freely given is rarely forgotten.

In the end, listening is not a skill to be mastered.

It is a habit to be practiced.

A posture to be maintained.

A discipline to be renewed.

And through it, the steward preserves the humanity of the work.

There is a kind of confidence that comes not from speaking, but from staying.

From remaining present when answers are not yet clear.

From allowing another person the dignity of time.

The steward learns that this confidence is quiet, but it is strong.

It does not impress the room.

It steadies it.

In a profession increasingly measured by speed, listening becomes an act of resistance.

It resists reduction.

It resists simplification.

It resists the erosion of care.

And in that resistance, the steward preserves something rare.

A space where people are not rushed into decisions they do not yet understand.

Over decades, this posture shapes a life's work.

It shapes a reputation that cannot be manufactured.

It shapes trust that does not depend on performance, but on presence.

The steward who listens well is sought, not because they speak loudly, but because they hear deeply.

And when the career draws long, and the numbers have faded, and the volume is no longer counted, what remains is this:

The knowledge that one's words did not harm.

The knowledge that one's counsel protected.

The knowledge that one's attention mattered.

This is the reward of listening.

This is the dignity of the steward's way.

There is a moment in every professional's work when silence is no longer enough.

Listening has been done. Understanding has been formed. The facts are known.

Now comes the heavier task.

To speak.

Counsel is not information.

It is responsibility.

It is the willingness to place your name, your conscience, and your reputation behind the words you offer.

The steward does not merely present options.

They provide direction.

Many professionals hide behind neutrality.

They offer choices without guidance.

They provide data without interpretation.

They avoid the discomfort of recommendation by calling it objectivity.

But objectivity without care becomes abdication.

The steward does not abandon people to complexity.

They walk with them through it.

To counsel well requires courage.

The courage to say what may not be popular.

The courage to slow a decision that feels urgent.

The courage to challenge assumptions that feel comfortable.

The courage to disappoint in the short term in order to protect in the long.

There are moments when the steward must advise against what the client wants.

Not because the client is wrong.

But because the consequence is heavier than it appears.

This is where the profession reveals its integrity.

Not in the ease of agreement.

But in the difficulty of dissent.

A Conversation That Changed the Relationship

There are conversations that alter the course of trust.

They are not dramatic.

They are quiet.

A steward sits across from a client who is eager, confident, and certain.

The numbers work. The choice seems clear. The momentum is strong.

And yet, the steward hesitates.

Not out of fear.

But out of responsibility.

They speak carefully.

They explain the risk that is being underestimated.

They name the consequence that is being ignored.

The room grows uncomfortable.

Agreement fades.

Tension rises.

This is the moment where counsel proves its worth.

The client may resist.

They may disagree.

They may even leave.

But the steward remains faithful to the weight of the work.

Silence is safer than this.

But safety is not the steward's aim.

Protection is.

There is no applause for this work.

No recognition.

Often, not even agreement.

And yet, this is the heart of stewardship.

The Cost of Moral Courage

To counsel well is to accept the cost of disagreement.

To bear the discomfort of tension.

To remain present when trust is tested.

The steward does not escape this cost.

They accept it.

They understand that courage is not loud.

It is steady.

The steward's counsel is not perfect.

Mistakes will be made.

Judgment will sometimes fall short.

But integrity is not the absence of error.

It is the presence of care.

Over time, the steward begins to understand that their greatest value is not in what they sell.

It is in what they prevent.

In the losses that never happen.

In the regrets that never surface.

In the harm that never materializes.

This is invisible work.

But it is sacred.

There are careers built on volume.

And there are careers built on trust.

Only one endures.

A profession that stops offering counsel becomes a marketplace of options.

A profession that offers counsel remains a guardian of consequence.

The steward preserves this guardianship.

In time, those who are counseled well begin to recognize it.

Not always immediately.

Sometimes only after years have passed.

Sometimes only after difficulty has been endured.

But recognition comes.

Trust deepens.

And relationship strengthens.

The Courage to Stand Alone

There will be moments when the steward stands alone in their recommendation.

When consensus is absent.

When pressure is high.

When compromise is tempting.

In these moments, the steward remembers who they serve.

Not the system.

Not the transaction.

But the person.

The courage to counsel is the courage to be responsible.

It is the courage to be affected.

It is the courage to stand inside the weight of the work.

And it is this courage that defines the steward.

There are days when the steward leaves the office with a heaviness that cannot be measured.

Not because the work was difficult.

But because it was faithful.

They said what needed to be said, not what was easiest to say.

They stood where it would have been simpler to step aside.

They bore the discomfort of another's disappointment in order to protect their future.

This weight is rarely acknowledged.

But it is the cost of integrity.

There are also moments when the steward must counsel not only against a decision, but against a mindset.

Against haste.

Against overconfidence.

Against the belief that risk can be ignored because the present feels strong.

This is the quiet work of leadership.

And leadership, in this profession, is rarely titled.

It is practiced.

The steward soon learns that courage is not an act.

It is a habit.

It is formed in small decisions, repeated over years, until the posture of integrity becomes natural.

Until counsel is offered not as confrontation, but as care.

There will be times when the steward's counsel is not followed.

When the client chooses the easier path.

When consequence eventually arrives.

In those moments, the steward feels a grief that is professional, but also deeply human.

Not because they were right.

But because harm might have been prevented.

This grief is part of the calling.

Yet there are also moments of quiet vindication.

When years pass.

When difficulty is endured.

When a client returns and says, "You were right to warn me."

These words are not spoken often.

But when they are, they carry more weight than praise.

This is the reward of moral courage.

Not recognition.

But trust.

And trust, earned this way, is lasting

There will come a day when the numbers no longer matter.

The volume fades. The rankings disappear. The metrics are forgotten.

What remains is the impact.

Not the impact that can be charted.

But the impact that is felt.

A career is not finally measured by how much was produced.

It is measured by how much was protected.

By the families who endured. By the losses that did not destroy. By the futures that remained intact.

This is the steward's accounting.

And it is very different from the world's.

The steward does not build monuments.

They build stability.

They do not chase recognition.

They cultivate trust.

And trust, once earned, outlives the transaction.

There are people who will never know the full value of what was done for them.

Because nothing bad happened.

Because crisis was avoided.

Because protection worked.

This is the steward's quiet triumph.

And it is the highest form of service.

There is a deep humility in this kind of work.

It teaches the professional that significance is often invisible.

That the greatest successes are those that leave no scars.

That the highest form of service is prevention.

Over time, the steward learns that the best work often looks like nothing at all.

No headlines. No emergencies. No regret.

Only continuity. Only peace. Only the ordinary blessing of stability.

A lifetime in this profession reveals a pattern.

The conversations that were slowed. The recommendations that were difficult. The counsel that was resisted, but later understood.

These moments do not appear on reports. But they shape lives. They become the quiet architecture of another family's future.

There are seasons when the steward wonders if the work is noticed.

When effort feels unseen. When care feels unmeasured. When integrity feels inefficient.

In these seasons, doubt whispers that volume is all that matters.

That speed is success. That growth is proof. That numbers are truth.

But the steward learns, slowly and sometimes painfully, that what endures is not volume, but virtue.

Not performance, but presence. Not production, but protection.

Legacy is not built in moments of triumph.

It is built in seasons of faithfulness. In the quiet consistency of care. In the repeated choice to protect rather than perform.

It is built in the thousands of small, unseen decisions where the steward chooses restraint over impulse, counsel over convenience, and responsibility over reward.

When the career draws long, and the work is reviewed not by metrics but by memory, this is what remains:

Not the deals closed. But the people served. Not the revenue earned. But the responsibility carried. Not the recognition received. But the trust preserved.

There is a peace that comes with this accounting.

A peace that does not depend on applause. A peace that does not require recognition. A peace that rests in the knowledge that the work was worthy of the trust placed in it.

This peace cannot be purchased. It is earned. Slowly. Faithfully. Over time.

The steward's reward is not fame.

It is rest. It is the quiet confidence that one's words did not harm. That one's counsel protected. That one's attention mattered. It is the knowledge that when the moment of consequence arrived, the steward stood where they should have stood.

There is a kind of professional poverty that comes from chasing only results. And there is a kind of professional wealth that comes from preserving people.

The steward chooses the second. Again and again.

A profession that remembers this will endure. A profession that forgets it will hollow.

For when protection becomes secondary, the soul of the work erodes. And when the soul erodes, the profession may still function, but it will no longer serve.

The steward understands that they are not merely practicing a trade. They are carrying a trust. They are standing between risk and ruin. They are holding a quiet line of defense for people who may never fully understand how close they once were to loss.

This is not glamorous work. But it is holy work.

There are men and women who will never stand on a stage.

They will never be recognized by title. They will never be quoted.

Yet their work will echo quietly through generations.

The steward is one of these.

Their influence is not loud. It is enduring.

Consider the family that remains in their home after loss. The business that survives a season that could have ended it. The widow who sleeps at night because provision was made long before grief arrived.

These outcomes do not appear in annual reports. But they are the true measure of the work.

The steward often does not witness the full consequence of their care.

They plant seeds whose shade they will never sit under. They build defenses they will never see tested. They prepare for storms that may never come.

And yet, this is the nobility of the calling.

In a culture obsessed with immediacy, stewardship is patient. It believes in tomorrow. It plans beyond the present. It values durability over display.

There is a spiritual dimension to this labor, whether named or not. To stand between vulnerability and harm is to participate in protection.

To preserve another's peace is to practice mercy. To guard another's future is to exercise responsibility at its highest form.

When the steward is tired, when the years have accumulated, when the work has demanded more than it returned, this truth remains:

What was protected mattered. Who was served mattered. And that is enough.

And when the final measure is taken, when the career is no longer active and the ledger is no longer kept, the steward's legacy will not be written in numbers.

It will be written in names.

In families who remained whole. In futures that were preserved. In peace that was protected.

This is the inheritance of stewardship. This is the dignity of the calling.

And in the end, this is the measure that remains.

"A man who does not think for himself does not think at all."

Oscar Wilde

CHAPTER 6: Why Quotas Never Built A Community

Communities are not built by targets. They are built by trust, sustained by presence, and strengthened by shared responsibility over time. Quotas were never designed to do any of these things. They were designed to measure output. And in that simple distinction lies one of the quiet misunderstandings that reshaped the modern culture of insurance sales.

Quotas are not evil. In fact, they are useful tools. They clarify expectations. They make activity visible. They allow organizations to forecast growth and monitor performance. For companies responsible for managing risk and capital, those things matter. Measurement introduces discipline, and discipline can protect an organization from chaos.

But usefulness and virtue are not the same thing.

Quotas measure activity, not integrity. They measure completion, not care. They measure production, not protection.

When the insurance profession first took shape, the work was guided less by measurement and more by responsibility. Agents understood that every policy carried a promise. That promise was not abstract. It was tied to real families, real livelihoods, and moments of vulnerability that could arrive without warning.

The early professional understood something simple but profound: the value of the work was revealed not at the moment of sale, but at the moment of loss.

That understanding shaped how the work was approached. Conversations were slower. Questions were deeper. Advice was given carefully because the consequences of that advice would eventually arrive in the real lives of the people sitting across the table.

Measurement changed the center of gravity.

Once numbers became the dominant signal of success, the work slowly reorganized itself around them. Not because professionals suddenly cared less, but because systems teach behavior more powerfully than intention ever could.

When a system rewards volume, volume increases. When it rewards speed, speed becomes the priority. When it rewards production cycles, conversations compress themselves to fit those cycles.

None of this requires bad people. It requires only repetition.

Over time the professional posture changes. Instead of beginning every conversation with the question, "What does this person truly need?" another quieter question begins to surface in the back of the mind:

"How does this decision affect my numbers?"

Most professionals would never say that question out loud. Many would be uncomfortable even admitting that it exists. But incentives shape behavior quietly. They do not require declaration. They only require consistency.

The longer someone works inside a system that measures them primarily by output, the more naturally their behavior aligns with that measurement.

This is what might be called the category error of quota culture. Organizations began asking quotas to do work they were never meant to do. They expected numbers to inspire loyalty. They expected targets to produce patience. They expected production goals to build trust.

But trust grows slowly.

A client remembers when you stayed longer than necessary. They remember when you advised them against a purchase that would have benefited you. They remember when you showed up after a storm not to sell anything, but simply to make sure they were alright.

None of those moments improve a quarterly report.

Yet those are the moments that create communities.

Communities emerge from consistent character, not efficient cycles. People begin to rely on one another when patterns of care repeat themselves over time. That repetition creates confidence. Confidence becomes trust. Trust eventually becomes loyalty.

Quotas operate on a different clock.

They reset every cycle. Every quarter begins with the same scoreboard cleared and ready again. Performance is recalculated. Rankings reshuffle. Urgency returns. Momentum must continue.

In this environment relationships struggle to mature because attention is continually redirected toward the next target.

Professionals begin living inside two timelines at once.

The first timeline belongs to the relationship. It moves slowly and unevenly. Trust develops through seasons. Understanding deepens through shared experience. Advice becomes more accurate because it rests on memory.

The second timeline belongs to the organization. It moves quickly and predictably. Cycles close. Reports are generated. Targets are reassigned. The next objective arrives.

The tension between these two timelines creates much of the quiet discomfort many professionals feel but rarely articulate.

Most people who enter the insurance profession do not do so because they are fascinated by production metrics. They enter because the work carries meaning. They believe helping families prepare for uncertainty is important. They believe guiding business owners through risk is worthwhile. They want their work to matter beyond the size of a commission.

But systems rarely measure meaning.

They measure results.

And so professionals adapt. Not because they abandon their values, but because they learn what the system recognizes. Listening becomes shorter. Conversations become structured. Recommendations become quicker. Advice sometimes arrives before understanding is fully formed.

This is not the result of unethical people. It is the result of powerful incentives.

Behavior follows reward.

And reward, in most modern sales environments, follows numbers.

The tragedy is that the original craft of salesmanship already contained its own discipline. It required patience, observation, and judgment. A skilled professional knew when to wait. They knew when fear was speaking louder than reason. They knew when a client needed time rather than persuasion.

That kind of judgment cannot be forced into a metric.

It exists only inside the professional themselves.

Historically, communities were built by individuals rather than systems. The banker who knew your name was not following a customer experience protocol. The agent who sat at your kitchen table was not executing a relationship management workflow. They were practicing responsibility.

Responsibility is personal.

It cannot be delegated to software or perfectly captured in a spreadsheet.

This does not mean quotas must disappear. Organizations require structure. Growth requires visibility. Discipline requires measurement.

But measurement must understand its limits.

Quotas can reveal how much work was completed. They cannot reveal how well people were served. They can track production. They cannot measure conscience.

When those two truths are confused, something subtle begins to erode.

The profession still functions. Policies are written. Companies grow. Careers continue.

But the quiet community that once surrounded the work becomes thinner.

Relationships feel more transactional. Trust takes longer to build. Loyalty becomes fragile. Professionals begin to feel interchangeable rather than relied upon.

The difference between being relied upon and being replaceable is one of the quiet dividing lines of professional life.

When someone is relied upon, their judgment matters. Their presence carries weight. Their absence is felt.

When someone is replaceable, the system simply finds another person to fill the role.

Quotas cannot determine which of these a professional becomes. Only behavior can.

The future of the profession will not be decided by whether measurement exists. Measurement will always exist.

The real question is whether professionals remember that their responsibility extends beyond what the measurement captures.

Communities are not built by numbers.

They are built by people who believe their work carries consequences long after the report is filed and the quarter is closed.

Quotas can track the work.

Only professionals can carry the responsibility.

In earlier generations of the profession, leadership looked different than it does today.

Leaders were not primarily measured by the numbers their teams produced. They were measured by the people they formed. Their task was not simply to drive output, but to shape judgment. They taught younger agents how to listen, how to slow down, and how to carry the responsibility that came with advising another family about risk.

Leadership, in those days, resembled mentorship more than management.

A young agent did not begin by chasing production. They began by watching someone who had already carried the weight of the work. They listened to conversations. They sat quietly in meetings. They learned how experienced professionals asked questions before offering answers.

This process was rarely formal.

It happened through observation. Through repetition. Through trust slowly extended by someone who had already proven they understood the craft.

The experienced agent did not simply teach how to sell a policy. They taught when not to.

They showed how to recognize fear disguised as urgency. They showed how to pause when a client felt overwhelmed. They showed how to recognize that sometimes the most responsible advice was to wait.

This kind of formation cannot happen quickly.

It requires patience from the mentor and humility from the apprentice. It requires time spent together in real situations where judgment must be exercised rather than memorized.

For much of the profession's history, this quiet apprenticeship formed the backbone of ethical salesmanship.

But apprenticeship requires something that modern quota culture struggles to provide: time.

When leadership becomes responsible primarily for hitting production targets, time changes value. Every hour must be justified. Every conversation must contribute toward visible output. Activities that do not translate quickly into measurable performance slowly disappear.

Mentorship is often one of the first casualties.

It is difficult to measure the value of sitting with a young agent while they struggle through their first difficult client conversation. It is difficult to quantify the benefit of explaining why a recommendation should be delayed rather than rushed.

Those moments may shape an entire career, but they do not appear easily in performance reports.

So organizations gradually reframe leadership itself.

Instead of mentors, they create managers.

Managers track activity. They monitor dashboards. They review production metrics. They provide feedback primarily in response to numbers rather than situations.

This change is not necessarily malicious. Many managers want to support their teams. But the environment surrounding them reshapes their priorities. When leadership is evaluated primarily by team production, leaders naturally focus on the behaviors most likely to influence those numbers.

The conversation shifts.

Instead of asking, "How did that conversation with the client unfold?" leaders begin asking, "How many policies did we write this week?"

Instead of exploring why a client hesitated, they review why a sale was lost.

Instead of discussing judgment, they discuss performance.

None of these discussions are inherently wrong. But they subtly redefine what success looks like.

Over time, younger agents internalize these signals.

They begin to believe that mastery of the profession means mastering the metrics. They assume that the fastest way to prove their value is through volume rather than wisdom.

The craft of listening becomes secondary to the urgency of producing.

This transformation changes how knowledge moves through the profession.

When mentorship fades, learning becomes procedural rather than experiential. New agents are trained through manuals, scripts, and digital training modules. These tools can convey information effectively, but they struggle to transmit judgment.

Judgment is learned through stories.

It is formed when an experienced professional explains why a certain recommendation felt wrong, even though it might have been profitable. It is developed when someone shares the memory of a claim that could have been prevented if they had listened more carefully.

Those kinds of lessons rarely fit inside training modules.

They are passed from person to person.

When the system prioritizes speed over formation, those stories are told less often. The profession becomes technically efficient but morally thinner.

Younger professionals still learn how to close a sale. But they are less likely to learn how to recognize the moments when closing a sale would violate the spirit of the work.

This shift does not mean modern professionals lack integrity. Many care deeply about serving clients well.

But integrity requires guidance.

Without mentors to model responsible judgment, young professionals must rely on the signals provided by the system around them. If the system praises production above all else, they naturally orient themselves toward production.

In time, the culture of the profession begins to mirror the incentives that shape it.

Leaders who wish to mentor discover that mentorship must happen in small, unofficial moments. It happens in brief conversations between meetings. It happens quietly after a difficult interaction when someone takes the time to explain what really mattered in that exchange.

These moments still exist.

They persist wherever experienced professionals refuse to reduce the craft entirely to numbers.

But they are harder to sustain in environments where leadership is measured primarily by output.

The difference between a manager and a mentor is subtle but profound.

A manager asks, "Did we meet the goal?"

A mentor asks, "Did we do the work well?"

The first question evaluates performance.

The second forms character.

Both questions have a place in a functioning organization. But when the first dominates entirely, the second slowly disappears from the conversation.

And when that happens, the profession loses something difficult to recover.

Not skill.

Skill can be taught quickly.

What disappears is wisdom.

Wisdom develops slowly. It emerges from years of seeing how advice plays out in real lives. It forms when someone reflects on both their successes and their mistakes, and then passes those lessons to the next generation.

Without that transfer of wisdom, every generation begins again as if the profession were new.

They learn the mechanics quickly. They master the tools. But the deeper understanding of responsibility takes much longer to emerge, and sometimes never fully does.

This is why the structure surrounding leadership matters so much.

If organizations want professionals who understand the weight of their work, they must create environments where experienced voices still shape younger ones.

Not through dashboards alone, but through presence.

Through conversation.

Through example.

Because communities are not built by systems.

They are built by people who teach one another how to carry responsibility.

And leadership, at its best, is simply the practice of helping others grow into that responsibility.

Every profession is shaped not only by what it rewards, but by what it quietly punishes.

In a quota-driven culture, the most powerful force is often not ambition. It is fear.

Fear rarely appears openly in the language of the workplace. Organizations speak instead about goals, performance, growth, and accountability. These are reasonable concepts. They belong in any serious profession. But beneath those words another emotional current often develops, one that professionals feel long before they ever describe it.

The current is pressure.

Pressure to meet numbers. Pressure to stay ahead of peers. Pressure to prove one's value repeatedly.

Over time, pressure changes how decisions are made.

The professional who once approached each conversation with calm curiosity begins to feel the invisible clock ticking behind every interaction. Time becomes compressed. Conversations become directional. Instead of slowly uncovering what a client truly needs, the professional begins guiding the conversation toward outcomes that satisfy both the client and the production requirement waiting in the background.

Again, this does not happen because professionals abandon their integrity.

It happens because fear is a powerful motivator.

A young agent who misses their numbers for several months begins to feel uncertainty about their future. A manager whose team struggles to produce feels the weight of expectations from above. Even experienced professionals can feel the quiet pressure to maintain the momentum they have built over the years.

Fear rarely shouts.

It whispers.

It whispers questions like:

"Am I falling behind?" "Will this conversation lead to something?" "Can I afford to spend more time here?"

Those questions slowly reshape behavior.

Service, in its purest form, requires patience. It requires a willingness to explore a client's situation without knowing exactly where the conversation will lead. It requires listening deeply enough to understand fears that the client may not even articulate clearly.

Fear shortens that process.

Under pressure, professionals begin to guide conversations toward clarity faster than clarity naturally arrives. They help clients make decisions quickly because speed reduces uncertainty. The conversation remains polite. The recommendation may still be reasonable. But something subtle has changed.

The professional is no longer fully free.

Part of their attention remains fixed on the invisible scoreboard measuring the outcome of the interaction.

Over time this tension becomes emotionally exhausting.

Most people enter the insurance profession because they believe the work matters. They believe helping families prepare for uncertainty carries genuine responsibility. When they discover that their environment constantly pushes them toward speed rather than understanding, a quiet internal conflict begins.

They want to serve well.

But they also need to survive inside the system that measures them.

This tension rarely leads to dramatic ethical failures. Instead, it produces something more subtle: gradual compromise.

The professional begins shortening conversations that deserve more time. They begin accepting recommendations that are good enough rather than carefully searching for the best solution. They begin interpreting hesitation as an obstacle rather than a signal that more understanding is needed.

None of these choices feel catastrophic in isolation.

But the accumulation of them slowly reshapes the character of the profession.

Fear also affects how professionals relate to one another.

In an environment dominated by production metrics, colleagues become competitors. Everyone understands that performance rankings exist, even when they are not formally published. Recognition, bonuses, and opportunities tend to follow those who produce the most.

Competition can inspire excellence.

But when competition is constant, collaboration becomes fragile.

Professionals hesitate to share insights that might help someone else surpass them. Conversations between colleagues become guarded. The sense that everyone is working together to protect the community slowly fades.

Instead of a profession built on shared responsibility, the environment begins to resemble a marketplace of individual performers.

The irony is that the original spirit of insurance was deeply communal.

Early insurance organizations formed precisely because individuals understood they were stronger together than apart. Risk was shared. Responsibility was shared. Protection was shared.

Fear reverses that instinct.

It isolates.

It encourages individuals to focus first on their own security rather than the health of the broader professional community.

This shift also affects how clients perceive the profession.

Clients are remarkably sensitive to emotional signals. Even when professionals speak carefully, subtle cues reveal whether the conversation is guided by patience or urgency. A hurried tone, a slightly rushed explanation, or an eagerness to conclude the conversation can signal that something other than the client's needs may be influencing the interaction.

Trust erodes slowly when those signals accumulate.

A client may not accuse the professional of wrongdoing. They may not even fully articulate their discomfort. But they begin to feel that the relationship is more transactional than personal.

Once that perception takes root, rebuilding trust becomes difficult.

The professional may still be competent. The policy may still be appropriate. But the deeper confidence that once defined the profession begins to weaken.

Fear also alters the emotional experience of the professional themselves.

In environments where service is the primary guiding principle, professionals often feel pride in their work. They believe their judgment matters. They see the results of their advice play out in the lives of their clients. When a difficult claim occurs and the protection works as intended, the professional experiences a quiet sense of fulfillment.

But in environments dominated by constant pressure, that pride becomes harder to sustain.

Success begins to feel temporary.

A strong month of production provides relief rather than satisfaction. The next cycle begins immediately. The scoreboard resets. The professional finds themselves starting over again.

This constant reset makes it difficult for professionals to step back and recognize the deeper meaning of their work.

They begin measuring themselves the same way the system measures them: by the numbers they produce.

When that happens, something profound is lost.

The profession was never meant to define its practitioners by production alone.

It was meant to define them by responsibility.

Responsibility to clients. Responsibility to communities. Responsibility to the promises contained inside every policy written.

Fear cannot sustain that responsibility.

Fear narrows attention. It focuses on immediate outcomes rather than long-term consequences. It encourages professionals to solve today's pressure rather than tomorrow's risk.

Service, by contrast, expands attention.

It invites professionals to consider the future lives of the families they advise. It encourages patience. It allows conversations to unfold naturally because the goal is not speed but understanding.

The challenge facing the profession today is not simply to produce more efficiently.

It is to recover the freedom necessary to serve well.

Professionals must once again feel able to slow down when the situation requires it. They must feel secure enough to recommend patience rather than urgency. They must remember that the most valuable moments in their work are often the ones that never appear in any report.

A conversation that prevents a mistake.

Advice that protects a family years later.

A relationship built slowly enough that trust becomes natural rather than negotiated.

Those moments rarely satisfy a quota.

But they are the moments that rebuild a profession.

And the professionals who rediscover the courage to prioritize service over fear will quietly become the ones communities rely on again.

"The time is always right to do what is right"

Martin Luther King Jr.

CHAPTER 7: The Small-Town Cure

In many corners of the country, the insurance profession has changed dramatically.

Technology has accelerated communication. Large organizations have centralized operations. Sales

processes have been refined, automated, and optimized.

These developments have created efficiencies that earlier generations could scarcely imagine.

But while the industry has modernized, something interesting has quietly remained unchanged in many

small communities.

The profession still looks remarkably familiar.

Walk into a small-town insurance office and you may notice something that feels almost out of step with

the modern pace of the world.

People still know one another.

The agent may have gone to school with the client sitting across the desk. They may attend the same

church. Their children may play on the same baseball team. Conversations often begin with something other than insurance.

"How is your mother doing?" "Did the rain help your crops this year?" "Are the kids enjoying their new

school?"

To an outsider, this might look inefficient.

But to the people involved, it is simply normal.

These conversations are not distractions from the work.

They are the foundation of it.

Insurance has always been built on trust, and trust grows more naturally in environments where people actually know one another. When an agent understands the rhythms of the community, they also

understand the risks that surround it.

They know which families are expanding their businesses. They know which farms have struggled

through a difficult season. They know which young families are buying their first homes.

This knowledge cannot be downloaded from a database.

It comes from living alongside the people you serve.

In these environments, the professional relationship feels different.

Clients are not anonymous policyholders.

They are neighbors.

That simple distinction changes how the work is approached.

An agent advising a neighbor does not think primarily about closing a sale. They think about the

consequences that recommendation will carry when they see that same person at the grocery store, at

church, or at the school football game on Friday night.

Accountability becomes personal.

And personal accountability naturally encourages careful judgment.

There is also something deeper happening in those conversations —
something that cannot easily be

measured by modern systems.

There is history.

When two people sit across from one another in a small community,
they often share years of memory.

They remember seasons of prosperity and seasons of hardship. They
remember storms that damaged

crops, fires that threatened businesses, or accidents that changed the
course of a family's life.

Those memories shape the way protection is discussed.

Insurance stops being an abstract product and becomes something far
more human.

It becomes a promise.

A promise that if the unexpected happens, the family sitting across the
desk will not face that moment

alone.

Small-town agents also operate under a different form of reputation.

In large cities, reputations can sometimes be shaped by marketing.

In small communities, reputations are shaped by stories.

One good experience travels quickly.

So does one bad one.

Because the community is tightly connected, the professional quickly learns that every

recommendation contributes to a reputation that will either strengthen or weaken over time.

This creates a powerful incentive to serve well.

Not because a company requires it.

But because the community remembers it.

The small-town model also preserves something that many modern systems struggle to maintain:

continuity.

An agent may serve the same family for decades.

They may insure a young couple when they purchase their first home, later protect the business that

couple builds, and eventually help insure the next generation as the children grow into adulthood.

Over time, the agent becomes more than a salesperson.

They become a trusted advisor whose understanding of the family deepens year after year.

This long-term perspective changes the nature of advice.

When a professional expects to serve someone for decades, short-term thinking makes little sense.

Recommendations must stand the test of time because the relationship itself is built on time.

It is tempting to assume that the small-town model survives only because of nostalgia or tradition.

But the truth is more practical than that.

The model survives because it works.

Communities function better when people trust the professionals who serve them.

Businesses make better decisions when they have advisors who understand their circumstances

deeply.

Families face uncertainty with greater confidence when they know someone knowledgeable is guiding

them through complicated choices.

The presence of trusted professionals strengthens the stability of the entire community.

Insurance, when practiced in this way, becomes more than a transaction.

It becomes a form of quiet stewardship.

Stewardship does not require grand gestures.

It appears in ordinary moments.

It appears when an agent spends an extra hour explaining a coverage decision to a young family

buying their first home.

It appears when a business owner calls their agent before making an important decision because they

trust that the advice will be honest.

It appears when an agent shows up after a storm, not with a sales pitch, but with reassurance that the

protection in place will do what it was designed to do.

These moments rarely appear in production reports.

But they are the moments that build communities.

And wherever those moments still happen, the spirit of the insurance profession is still alive.

The Kitchen Table Conversation

There is a moment in many insurance careers that quietly changes how a professional sees the work.

It is the moment when the conversation moves beyond numbers. Beyond premiums, deductibles, and coverage forms. It is the moment when the client begins talking about their life.

In many offices across the country, that moment still happens around a kitchen table.

The setting itself changes the tone of the conversation.

A kitchen table is not a conference room. It is not a sales office. It is a place where families gather,

where decisions are made, and where life is discussed honestly.

When a professional sits at that table, the conversation naturally becomes more personal.

The walls of the home tell a story. There are photographs of children growing up. There may be a

calendar marked with family events. A dog wanders through the room and settles quietly in the corner.

These small details remind everyone involved that the discussion taking place is not abstract.

It is about real lives.

The experienced professional understands that the most important part of this conversation is not

speaking.

It is listening.

Listening carefully enough to understand what the client is actually worried about.

Sometimes those concerns are obvious.

A young couple buying their first home worries about protecting the future they are just beginning to

build.

A business owner worries about the employees who rely on the company they have spent years

creating.

A parent worries about the stability of their family if something unexpected were to happen.

These worries rarely appear on an application.

But they are the reason the conversation matters.

In many ways, the kitchen-table conversation represents the opposite of the rushed sales environment

that has become common in some parts of the industry.

There is no script.

There is no countdown timer.

There is only the slow process of understanding.

The professional asks questions.

How long have you lived here? What plans do you have for the business over the next few years? What

would concern you most if something unexpected happened?

These questions are not simply gathering information.

They are building context.

And context is what allows the professional to give advice that actually fits the life sitting across from

them.

One of the most important skills an insurance professional can develop is the ability to remain patient

during these conversations.

Many clients do not immediately articulate their real concerns.

They may begin by asking about price.

But price is rarely the whole story.

Often price is simply the first question people ask before they feel comfortable discussing the deeper

ones.

When the professional remains patient, something interesting often happens.

The conversation opens.

Clients begin to talk about the things that actually matter to them.

A couple may explain that they recently had a child and want to make sure their family would be secure

if something happened.

A business owner may reveal that they have taken on new debt to expand and worry about how the

company would survive a major loss.

These details transform the conversation.

Insurance stops being a product.

It becomes protection.

This is where the professional must exercise judgment.

The right recommendation does not come from memorizing a product brochure.

It comes from understanding the client's situation deeply enough to see what protection truly matters.

Sometimes the right answer involves recommending more coverage.

Sometimes it involves simplifying coverage.

And occasionally the right answer is simply explaining that the client is already protected well enough.

Kitchen-table conversations also create something else that is difficult to measure but incredibly valuable.

They create memory.

Years later, when a client faces a difficult situation, they remember the person who sat at that table and

took the time to understand their life.

They remember that the conversation was not rushed.

They remember that the advice felt thoughtful.

That memory becomes the foundation of trust.

And trust is what keeps the relationship intact long after the original policy was written.

The world may continue to move faster.

Technology will continue to evolve.

But the need for thoughtful conversations will never disappear.

Because behind every policy is still a human life.

And human lives cannot be fully understood through forms and algorithms alone.

They must be understood through conversation.

Where those conversations still happen, the profession still lives

The Reputation That Compounds

In the insurance business, people often speak about building a book of business.

The phrase sounds technical, almost mechanical, as if the work consists primarily of assembling policies inside a portfolio.

But anyone who has practiced the profession long enough knows that a book of business is something very different.

It is a collection of relationships.

Every policy inside that book represents a person who trusted the professional enough to accept their guidance. It represents a conversation that took place at a specific moment in time, when someone was trying to make sense of risk and uncertainty.

Over the years those moments accumulate.

And eventually the professional begins to notice something interesting.

The book grows not only because of sales.

It grows because of reputation.

Reputation moves quietly through communities.

Rarely through advertisements.

Rarely through formal announcements.

Instead it moves through conversations.

A neighbor mentions the agent who helped them understand their coverage after a difficult storm.

A business owner recommends the professional who took the time to walk through their risks carefully before writing the policy.

A young family shares the name of the person who explained their protection clearly when they purchased their first home.

None of these conversations are dramatic.

But they are powerful.

Because recommendations given between friends carry a kind of credibility that marketing cannot easily replicate.

Over time, this quiet network of conversations becomes the true engine of a professional career.

The agent who serves people well begins to receive calls from individuals they have never met before.

"Your name was given to us by a friend."

"We were told you might be able to help us understand our coverage."

"My neighbor said you took care of them after their claim."

These calls represent something far more meaningful than a new opportunity.

They represent trust that has already begun forming before the first conversation even takes place.

And that kind of trust changes the entire dynamic of the relationship.

When trust enters the conversation early, the professional no longer has to spend most of the meeting proving their credibility.

Instead they can spend their energy understanding the client.

They can ask deeper questions.

They can listen more carefully.

They can focus on giving thoughtful advice rather than persuading someone to believe they are qualified to offer it.

In this environment, the work becomes more fulfilling for everyone involved.

The client feels understood.

The professional feels respected.

And the relationship begins on a foundation strong enough to last for years.

This is why experienced agents often say that the most valuable asset in their career is not a product, a contract, or even a company relationship.

It is their reputation.

Reputation takes years to build.

But once established, it becomes remarkably durable.

A professional who consistently acts with integrity develops a reputation that can sustain them through difficult economic cycles.

Markets change.

Rates rise and fall.

Companies adjust their strategies.

But a professional known for honest advice continues to receive the one thing that matters most in this profession: the opportunity to help.

Reputation also changes the nature of growth.

Early in a career, growth often requires effort and persistence. The professional must introduce themselves to new people, explain their services, and earn the first layer of trust.

But as reputation develops, growth begins to feel different.

The community itself begins participating in the expansion of the book.

Satisfied clients become advocates.

Business owners introduce the agent to colleagues.

Families recommend the professional to relatives who are moving into the area.

The book grows organically because people believe the relationship will be valuable to those they care about.

This process creates something that is both professionally and personally rewarding.

The professional begins to realize that their work is woven into the life of the community.

They insure the first homes of young couples.

They help business owners protect companies that employ local families.

They assist older clients as they transition into retirement and begin thinking about the legacy they will leave behind.

Over time the professional becomes a familiar presence during important moments in people's lives.

That presence carries responsibility.

But it also carries meaning.

The remarkable thing about this kind of reputation is that it cannot be rushed.

No advertising campaign can manufacture it.

No sales technique can shortcut it.

Reputation grows only through consistent behavior over time.

Through conversations where the professional listens carefully.

Through recommendations that prioritize the client's future rather than the professional's immediate gain.

Through the quiet demonstration that the person offering advice genuinely cares about the outcome.

This is why the small-town model continues to teach the broader profession an important lesson.

It reminds us that trust compounds.

In the same way that financial investments grow slowly but steadily over time, reputations built on integrity accumulate value year after year.

A single honest conversation may not seem significant in the moment.

But thousands of those conversations over the course of a career create something extraordinary.

They create a professional who is known.

Known not simply as someone who sells insurance.

But as someone people rely on when the unexpected arrives.

And in a profession built around protecting people from uncertainty, there may be no greater achievement than that.

The Next Generation

Every profession eventually faces a question that cannot be answered by systems or technology.

The question is simple.

Who will carry the work forward?

Insurance, like many professions, now finds itself standing at that moment.

A large generation of experienced professionals is slowly stepping away from the work. Many of them

spent decades building relationships within their communities. They guided families through difficult

claims, advised business owners through uncertain seasons, and built reputations that stretched across

entire towns.

Those professionals did more than write policies.

They carried responsibility.

And now the profession must ask whether the next generation will carry that responsibility with the

same seriousness.

Much has been written about the challenges facing the insurance workforce.

Recruitment is difficult. Training new professionals takes time. Younger generations often see the

industry as complicated or outdated.

But those challenges tell only part of the story.

The deeper question is not whether new people will enter the profession.

It is how they will be formed once they arrive.

If new agents are trained primarily to chase numbers, the profession
will continue drifting toward the

transactional model that many communities already distrust.

But if new agents are formed as stewards of protection, something
very different can happen.

The profession can renew itself.

Formation matters.

Every young professional entering the industry begins with energy and
ambition. They want to succeed.

They want to prove themselves. They want to build something
meaningful.

What they become depends largely on what they see modeled around
them.

If they observe leaders who treat clients as transactions, they will
naturally adopt that posture.

If they observe professionals who listen patiently, explain carefully,
and accept responsibility for the

consequences of their advice, they will begin to imitate that behavior
instead.

This is how professional culture travels from one generation to the
next.

Not through policy manuals.

Through example.

The encouraging truth is that the spirit of the profession has never fully disappeared.

Across the country there are still offices where experienced agents quietly mentor younger colleagues.

They review policies together. They talk through difficult situations. They explain why certain

recommendations should never be rushed.

These moments of mentorship rarely appear in performance reports.

But they are the moments where the future of the profession is actually decided.

Because when a young professional learns to see insurance as a responsibility rather than a product,

their entire career takes on a different direction.

Clients sense this difference immediately.

People may not understand the details of every coverage form or endorsement. But they recognize

sincerity when they encounter it.

They recognize when someone is genuinely trying to protect them.

And they recognize when someone is simply trying to complete a transaction.

Over time, communities gravitate toward the professionals they trust.

Not the ones who speak the fastest. Not the ones who advertise the most aggressively.

The ones who consistently demonstrate that the promise behind the policy matters.

This is why the restoration of the profession will not come primarily from technology, regulation, or

corporate strategy.

It will come from professionals.

From individuals who choose to approach the work with patience and integrity.

From leaders who take the time to mentor rather than merely manage.

From agents who remember that every policy they write represents a promise that will one day be

tested by real life.

The next generation of insurance professionals therefore inherits more than an industry.

They inherit a reputation.

Some parts of that reputation have been weakened by years of rushed transactions and misunderstood

incentives.

But reputations can be rebuilt.

Slowly.

Conversation by conversation. Recommendation by recommendation. Relationship by relationship.

The small-town model reminds us how this rebuilding begins.

It begins when a professional chooses to know the people they serve.

When they choose to listen before advising.

When they understand that the success of their career will ultimately be measured not by the number of

policies written, but by the number of people who trust them when life becomes uncertain.

If enough professionals choose that path, something remarkable begins to happen.

Communities once again see the insurance agent not as a salesperson, but as a trusted guide through

complicated risks.

Young professionals begin to discover that the work carries meaning beyond commissions.

And the profession gradually rediscovers the dignity it once held in the communities it serves.

The cure for many of the profession's modern frustrations may not lie in new systems at all.

It may lie in remembering the simple principles that guided the work from the beginning.

Know the people you serve. Protect them carefully. Honor the promise behind every policy.

Where those principles remain alive, the insurance profession remains alive as well.

And wherever the next generation chooses to carry them forward, the quiet restoration of the profession

has already begun.

"He who is not courageous enough to take risks will accomplish nothing in life."

Muhammad Ali

CHAPTER 8: The Kitchen Table Revival

The World Grew More Complicated

For most of the twentieth century, the insurance profession moved at a slower pace.

Applications were written by hand. Policies arrived through the mail. Underwriting decisions could take

days or even weeks.

The work required patience. And because the work moved slowly, the conversations surrounding it

often moved slowly as well. Agents met clients face to face. They sat in living rooms and kitchens. They talked through risks carefully because both sides understood that the decision being made would

eventually be tested by real life.

Protection was not treated as a transaction.

It was treated as a responsibility.

Over time, however, the pace of the world began to accelerate.

Communication became faster. Information became easier to access. Transactions that once required

hours could now be completed in minutes.

Nearly every profession experienced this transformation, and insurance was no exception. Obtaining

coverage became easier than it had ever been before. Quotes could be generated quickly. Applications

could be submitted instantly. Consumers were told that protection could now be purchased with

unprecedented speed and convenience.

For many observers, this seemed to signal a major shift.

If obtaining a policy had become this simple, what role remained for the traditional insurance

professional?

The prediction appeared logical. Many believed the agent would slowly disappear.

For a time, that prediction seemed convincing. The industry began emphasizing efficiency above nearly

everything else. Faster quotes. Faster applications. Faster transactions.

Speed became the promise.

Convenience became the brand.

But as the world accelerated, something unexpected happened.

The transaction became easier.

The decision became harder.

Insurance did not become simpler as the world modernized. It became more complex. Families began

living more complicated financial lives. Homes contained more value. Businesses faced new forms of

exposure that earlier generations had never encountered.

Coverage options expanded.

Policies contained more variations.

Liability risks evolved as society itself evolved.

The result was an interesting contradiction. People could obtain coverage faster than ever before, yet

many of them were less certain than ever about whether that coverage actually protected them.

Speed solved one problem.

It created another.

When decisions become complicated, people begin searching for guidance. Not simply someone who

can complete the transaction, but someone who can help them understand the consequences of the

decision.

And that is where the professional quietly reenters the picture.

The role of the insurance professional was never simply to process paperwork. The true role was

always interpretation.

Interpreting risk. Interpreting coverage. Interpreting how the details inside a policy interact with the

realities of a client's life.

Those tasks require something systems alone cannot provide.

Judgment.

Judgment develops slowly. It forms through years of conversations, claims experiences, and lessons

learned from situations that did not unfold the way anyone expected.

An experienced professional begins to recognize patterns. They remember the business owner who

underestimated a certain exposure. They remember the family who faced a difficult moment and

discovered that the right protection had already been quietly arranged.

Those memories shape the advice they give in future conversations.

This is why the human advisor has not disappeared. In many ways, the growing complexity of modern

life has made thoughtful advisors more valuable than ever.

When the decision is simple, people are comfortable making it alone. But when the decision carries

serious consequences, most people prefer guidance.

They want someone who can explain the difference between options that appear similar but produce

very different outcomes.

They want someone who can translate technical language into practical decisions.

And perhaps most importantly, they want someone they can call when the unexpected finally arrives.

Consider a simple example that happens every day in communities across the country.

A young couple buys their first home. They are excited, but they are also overwhelmed by the number

of new responsibilities that arrive with that purchase.

Mortgage payments. Property taxes. Maintenance. Insurance.

They search online and quickly receive several quotes. One option is cheaper than the others. At first

glance the decision appears obvious.

Why pay more for something that seems the same?

But what the screen cannot explain is how those policies differ beneath the surface. It cannot explain

subtle differences in coverage limits. It cannot explain exclusions. It cannot explain how certain

decisions may affect them years later if a loss occurs.

Now imagine that same couple sitting down with a thoughtful professional.

The conversation begins slowly.

The agent asks about the home.

How old is the property? Are there plans for renovations? Do you expect to stay here long term?

As the conversation continues, the agent learns something important. The couple plans to renovate the

home over the next few years and start a small side business from one of the rooms.

Those details completely change the conversation.

Certain protections become more important. Other options become less relevant.

The final recommendation may cost slightly more than the cheapest option they saw online. But it

protects the life they are actually building, not the simplified version represented on a screen.

Years later a storm damages the property. Because the earlier conversation took time to understand their plans, the coverage responds correctly. The house is repaired and the couple moves forward

without financial devastation.

In that moment the value of the earlier conversation becomes clear.

The difference was never speed.

The difference was understanding.

Moments like this rarely appear in industry reports, but they happen every day in offices where

professionals still approach the work as a responsibility rather than a transaction.

And each time they occur, they quietly remind the profession of its original purpose:

To stand beside people when life becomes uncertain.

Why People Still Want Someone to Call

In theory, modern consumers have more information than any generation that came before them.

A person can search almost any question and receive thousands of answers within seconds. Articles

explain financial planning. Videos describe insurance concepts. Comparison tools promise to sort

through options and display the best prices available.

From a distance, it might appear that people no longer need guidance at all.

But something interesting happens when information becomes overwhelming.

Clarity becomes harder to find.

The modern consumer is not suffering from a lack of information.

They are suffering from an abundance of it.

Search results rarely agree with one another. One article emphasizes cost savings. Another warns

about coverage gaps. One advisor suggests raising deductibles. Another insists the safest approach is

to lower them.

Each piece of information may be correct within a certain context.

But most consumers are not looking for theoretical answers.

They are trying to make decisions about their own lives.

And that is where the limits of general information begin to appear.

A website can explain what a deductible is.

It cannot know whether a specific family has enough savings to comfortably absorb that deductible.

An article can describe the benefits of liability protection.

It cannot understand the specific risks faced by a particular business owner.

Online tools can calculate prices.

They cannot evaluate the countless personal factors that shape how much protection a person truly

needs.

Those decisions require context.

And context only emerges through conversation.

This is why the most meaningful conversations in insurance rarely begin with numbers.

They begin with questions.

Tell me about the home you purchased. How long have you owned your business? What matters most

to you if something unexpected happens?

These questions may seem simple.

But they open the door to understanding the life behind the policy.

And once that life becomes visible, the professional can begin offering advice that actually fits the

person sitting across the table.

In many ways, this kind of conversation resembles the way communities once solved problems long

before modern technology existed.

Neighbors talked with neighbors.

Local professionals listened carefully before offering guidance.

Decisions were made with the understanding that relationships would continue long after the immediate problem had been resolved.

This approach created something powerful.

Accountability.

When advice is given within the context of an ongoing relationship, the person offering that advice

carries responsibility for the outcome.

That responsibility naturally encourages thoughtfulness.

It encourages humility.

It encourages the professional to ask one more question before offering a recommendation.

Contrast that with the purely transactional model.

When the interaction ends the moment the purchase is complete, the relationship disappears as quickly

as it began.

There is no shared history.

No follow-up conversation.

No long-term accountability.

The transaction may have been efficient.

But efficiency alone rarely builds trust.

People instinctively understand this difference.

That is why even in a world filled with digital tools, consumers still search for someone they can call when a problem arises.

They want reassurance that a knowledgeable person will answer the phone.

They want to know that the voice on the other end understands their situation.

And they want confidence that the guidance they receive will be grounded in experience rather than

guesswork.

Consider the moment when a claim occurs.

This is the moment when insurance stops being theoretical.

A fire damages part of a home.

A storm destroys a roof.

A business experiences a loss that threatens its ability to operate.

At that moment, the person holding the policy is not thinking about how quickly the transaction originally

took place.

They are thinking about what happens next.

Who do they call?

Who will explain what to expect?

Who will help them navigate a process that suddenly feels complicated and overwhelming?

These questions reveal the quiet truth at the heart of the profession.

Insurance is not simply purchased.

It is relied upon.

And when people rely on something, they prefer not to face it alone.

This is why the most successful professionals in the industry often describe their work in terms that go

far beyond selling policies.

They speak about relationships.

They speak about responsibility.

They speak about the privilege of being trusted during some of the most difficult moments their clients

will ever face.

Those moments rarely appear in marketing materials.

But they define the real work of the profession.

The kitchen table remains a powerful symbol for this kind of relationship.

Not because every conversation literally happens around a kitchen table anymore.

But because the image represents something deeper.

It represents the place where people talk honestly about their lives.

Where difficult decisions are made carefully.

Where advice carries weight because it comes from someone who understands the people involved.

Technology has changed the tools used in the profession.

But it has not changed the human need for guidance.

People still want to speak with someone who understands risk well enough to help them avoid

unnecessary mistakes.

They still want reassurance that their protection was arranged thoughtfully.

And when uncertainty appears, they still want someone they trust to help them navigate what comes

next.

In that sense, the revival of the kitchen-table spirit may not be a return to the past at all.

It may simply be the profession rediscovering something that was always essential.

The understanding that protection begins with conversation.

And that conversation, when handled with care and integrity, becomes the foundation of trust that lasts

for generations.

The Professional as Interpreter

When most people think about insurance, they imagine policies, premiums, and paperwork.

They picture documents filled with unfamiliar language and numbers that must be compared carefully

before making a decision.

But the experienced professional understands that insurance has always been something more than a

collection of documents.

It is a language.

A language written in clauses, exclusions, limits, and endorsements.

And like any language, it requires interpretation.

The average consumer rarely reads an insurance policy from beginning to end.

Even if they attempt to do so, the language often feels distant from everyday life.

Terms are precise. Definitions are structured carefully. Entire sections are written to address situations

the reader may never have considered.

From a legal perspective, this precision is necessary.

But from the perspective of the person trying to protect their home or business, the language can feel

overwhelming.

That is where the professional enters the picture.

Not simply as someone who sells the policy.

But as someone who translates it.

Translation is not a mechanical task.

It requires understanding both sides of the conversation.

On one side is the policy itself — the technical structure designed to define how protection works.

On the other side is the life of the person seeking protection — their family, their business, their plans

for the future.

The professional stands between those two realities and connects them.

They take the technical language of coverage and explain how it applies to the life unfolding in front of

them.

When this work is done well, something important happens.

The policy stops being abstract.

It becomes understandable.

This ability to interpret risk develops slowly.

It cannot be rushed.

A new agent may understand the basic structure of coverage. They may know how to quote a policy or

submit an application.

But interpretation requires something deeper.

It requires experience.

Over time, professionals begin to see patterns that younger practitioners might overlook.

They remember the contractor who assumed his general liability policy covered a situation that later

proved more complicated.

They remember the family who discovered that a small difference in coverage limits carried enormous

consequences after a loss.

Each experience adds another layer of judgment.

And that judgment gradually becomes one of the most valuable assets the professional possesses.

Experienced advisors often describe their work in a way that surprises people outside the industry.

They say that the most important part of their job happens before a policy is ever written.

It happens during the conversation.

During the questions that reveal what the client is truly trying to protect.

What do you worry about most? What would happen if your business had to close for several months?

How long would your savings support your family if your home needed major repairs?

These questions are not asked to create anxiety.

They are asked to reveal reality.

Because only when the reality of risk is understood can the protection be designed properly.

In this sense, the professional does something remarkably valuable.

They help people imagine the future.

Not in dramatic or frightening ways, but in practical ones.

They help the client think through situations that are unlikely but possible.

Storms that damage property. Accidents that create liability. Unexpected interruptions that threaten the

stability of a business.

By considering these possibilities early, the professional allows the client to make decisions calmly

rather than react emotionally later.

This quiet preparation is one of the greatest services the profession provides.

There is another element to interpretation that is often overlooked.

Good professionals do not simply recommend more protection.

They recommend appropriate protection.

Sometimes that means encouraging a client to increase coverage where the risk is significant.

Other times it means explaining that a client is already well protected and does not need additional

expense.

This balance requires integrity.

Because the professional must be willing to give advice that prioritizes the client's long-term wellbeing

rather than the immediate transaction.

When clients sense that integrity, something important begins to grow.

Trust.

Trust is not created by perfect explanations or impressive credentials.

It is created when people believe the advisor sitting across from them is genuinely committed to their

best interest.

Once that trust exists, conversations change.

Clients ask deeper questions. They share more details about their lives and plans. They invite the

professional to become a long-term advisor rather than a one-time transaction.

And with each conversation, the relationship grows stronger.

This is why the most respected professionals in the industry often have careers that span decades

within the same communities.

Their work becomes woven into the lives of the people they serve.

They insure the first homes of young families. They advise entrepreneurs as their businesses grow.

They help long-time clients adjust their protection as retirement approaches.

Over the years the professional begins to see something remarkable.

The policies change. The companies may change.

But the relationships remain.

When the profession is practiced this way, the insurance agent becomes something closer to a guide.

Someone who understands the terrain of risk well enough to help others travel through it safely.

A guide does not walk the path for the traveler.

But they know where the hazards exist.

They know which decisions require caution.

And they know how to help others reach their destination without unnecessary loss.

In a world filled with information, the role of the guide becomes even more important.

Because information alone does not create wisdom.

Wisdom emerges when knowledge is combined with experience, patience, and judgment.

The professional who brings those qualities to the conversation offers something far more valuable

than speed.

They offer understanding.

And when people face decisions that affect their homes, their businesses, and their families,

understanding is exactly what they are searching for.

Remembering the Profession

Every profession eventually faces moments when it must decide what it truly wants to become.

Insurance is no different.

For decades the industry has wrestled with competing pressures. Efficiency demanded faster

transactions. Competition pushed companies to emphasize price above almost everything else.

Technology promised convenience that previous generations could scarcely imagine.

None of these forces were inherently harmful.

In many ways they improved the accessibility of insurance and allowed millions of people to obtain

protection more easily than before.

But along the way something subtle began to fade.

The understanding that insurance was never meant to be only a product.

It was meant to be a promise.

A promise is a powerful thing.

When people purchase insurance, they are not buying a physical object they can immediately hold in

their hands. They are purchasing an agreement that will only reveal its value at some unknown moment

in the future.

Sometimes that moment arrives quickly.

A storm damages a home. A car accident creates unexpected expenses. A business faces a loss that

threatens its stability.

Other times the moment may not arrive for decades.

But whenever it does arrive, the promise must hold.

And when that promise is tested, the people involved rarely remember how quickly the policy was

purchased.

They remember something far more important.

They remember whether they trusted the person who helped them arrange it.

This is why the kitchen table remains such a powerful symbol for the profession.

The kitchen table is where life happens.

Families gather there to discuss plans and solve problems. Important decisions are made in that space because it represents familiarity, honesty, and shared responsibility.

When insurance conversations reflect that same spirit, something remarkable begins to happen.

The work regains its dignity.

The agent stops being perceived merely as a salesperson.

Instead, the agent becomes a trusted advisor — someone invited into the decision-making process

because their judgment is valued.

Restoring this spirit does not require abandoning the modern world.

The tools of the profession will continue to evolve.

Communication will continue to accelerate.

But the heart of the work has always been human.

Understanding people. Understanding risk. Helping individuals and businesses make thoughtful

decisions about uncertain futures.

Those responsibilities cannot be replaced by convenience alone.

They require patience.

They require listening.

And above all, they require integrity.

Integrity has always been the quiet foundation of the insurance profession.

Clients rarely have the technical knowledge required to verify every detail of a policy on their own.

Instead they rely on the character of the professional advising them.

They rely on the belief that the person guiding them is acting in good faith.

This trust creates an enormous responsibility for those who choose to practice the profession seriously.

Because every recommendation made today may influence a family's financial security years into the

future.

That responsibility should never be treated lightly.

Yet when professionals accept that responsibility with humility, the rewards of the work become deeply

meaningful.

They see firsthand how thoughtful protection can stabilize families during difficult moments.

They watch businesses survive events that might otherwise have forced them to close their doors.

They witness communities recover from storms, accidents, and unexpected hardships.

These outcomes rarely appear in marketing materials.

But they represent the true purpose of the profession.

The encouraging truth is that the spirit of the profession has never disappeared entirely.

Across towns and cities, there are still offices where agents know their clients by name.

Where conversations take place with patience rather than urgency.

Where professionals remember that their reputation will be measured not by how many policies they

sell this month, but by how faithfully they serve the people who trust them.

In those places, the kitchen-table spirit is still alive.

And wherever that spirit remains alive, the profession itself remains alive as well.

The future of insurance will not be determined solely by companies, systems, or regulations.

It will be determined by the professionals who choose how the work will be practiced.

Each conversation presents a choice.

The choice between rushing through a transaction or taking the time to understand the person sitting

across the table.

The choice between recommending the quickest option or the most appropriate protection.

The choice between treating the policy as a product or honoring it as a promise.

These decisions may seem small in isolation.

But across thousands of conversations and years of practice, they shape the character of the

profession itself.

If enough professionals choose the path of stewardship, the quiet revival of the insurance profession

will already be underway.

Communities will once again see agents not as intermediaries to be bypassed, but as trusted guides

through complicated decisions.

Young professionals entering the industry will discover that the work offers more than financial

opportunity.

It offers the chance to protect the lives and livelihoods of the people around them.

And clients will rediscover something that earlier generations understood instinctively.

That the right advisor is not simply someone who helps them purchase insurance.

It is someone who helps them face uncertainty with confidence.

In that sense, the revival of the kitchen-table spirit may not be about returning to the past at all.

It may simply be about remembering what the profession was always meant to be.

A calling rooted in trust.

A responsibility grounded in integrity.

And a promise that, when honored faithfully, strengthens the communities it serves.

"Always do your best. What you plant now, will harvest later."

Og Mandino

CHAPTER 9: The Standard Bearers

The Quiet Responsibility

Every profession eventually produces two kinds of participants.

Those who pass through it.

And those who carry it.

Most people who enter an industry see it first as an opportunity. A career path. A way to provide for

their families and build a life.

There is nothing wrong with that motivation.

Work has always been one of the primary ways people create stability and purpose for themselves and

those they care about.

But over time, a small number of professionals begin to see their work differently.

They begin to recognize that they are not merely participating in a job.

They are participating in a tradition.

The insurance profession is filled with such traditions. Many of them are quiet and rarely written down.

They exist in the habits passed from mentor to apprentice. In the stories shared between colleagues

who have seen the profession tested in difficult moments.

These traditions teach lessons that cannot easily be learned from textbooks.

Lessons about responsibility.

Lessons about patience.

Lessons about the importance of listening carefully before offering advice.

When young professionals first enter the industry, the work often appears technical.

Policies must be understood. Procedures must be followed. Markets must be navigated.

But the longer a person remains in the profession, the more they realize that its deepest lessons are not technical at all.

They are human.

Insurance is not ultimately about policies.

It is about people.

Every policy represents a life in motion.

A family building its future.

A business owner pursuing a dream.

A community depending on the stability of the institutions that serve it.

The professional who understands this begins to see their work through a different lens.

They are no longer simply arranging coverage.

They are helping protect the fragile progress people make as they build their lives.

This realization creates a quiet responsibility.

The professional becomes aware that the advice they give today may influence events years into the

future.

A recommendation made casually can have serious consequences later.

But a recommendation made thoughtfully can prevent enormous hardship.

This is why experienced professionals often speak about the profession with a kind of reverence.

They have seen what happens when protection works.

And they have seen what happens when it fails.

Those experiences leave an impression.

The agent who has helped a family recover after a devastating fire never forgets the relief that appears

when the coverage responds properly.

The advisor who has watched a business survive a crisis because the right protections were in place

understands the power of preparation.

Moments like these remind the professional that their work carries weight far beyond the paperwork

involved.

Over time, some professionals begin to recognize something else.

They are not only responsible for serving their clients.

They are also responsible for preserving the profession itself.

Every generation inherits the profession from those who came before.

Mentors teach the next wave of agents how to approach the work.

They pass along stories that reveal both the successes and the mistakes that shaped their careers.

In doing so, they protect the standards that allow the profession to function with integrity.

Without those standards, the profession slowly loses its identity.

It becomes indistinguishable from any other transactional marketplace.

But when professionals actively preserve those standards, something remarkable happens.

The profession retains its dignity.

Clients recognize the difference.

Communities begin to trust the professionals who demonstrate that they understand the responsibility

they carry.

These individuals become what might be called the standard bearers of the profession.

They do not necessarily hold the highest titles.

They may not always produce the largest sales numbers.

But they quietly uphold the principles that define what the profession is meant to be.

Integrity.

Judgment.

Stewardship.

Service.

Standard bearers rarely announce themselves.

Their influence spreads through example rather than proclamation.

You see them in the way they speak with clients.

In the patience they demonstrate when explaining complicated ideas.

In the willingness they show to place the long-term wellbeing of a client above the short-term benefit of

a transaction.

Young professionals who encounter such mentors often remember those interactions for the rest of

their careers.

Because in those moments they are witnessing the profession practiced the way it was always

intended.

In many ways, the future of the insurance profession depends less on innovation than on imitation.

The next generation must see the work performed with integrity before they can replicate it.

They must witness professionals who approach the job with humility and seriousness.

They must observe how experienced advisors balance technical knowledge with human understanding.

When those examples are present, the profession naturally renews itself.

When they are absent, the profession gradually loses its compass.

This is why the quiet responsibility carried by experienced professionals matters so deeply.

They are not merely serving their current clients.

They are shaping the expectations of the generation that will follow them.

Every conversation with a younger colleague becomes an opportunity to demonstrate what the

profession stands for.

Every decision made with integrity becomes a lesson that someone else may one day repeat.

Seen through this lens, the profession becomes something larger than individual careers.

It becomes a chain of stewardship.

Each generation receives the profession from those who practiced it before.

Each generation must decide whether to strengthen it or weaken it before passing it along.

The encouraging truth is that throughout the history of insurance, there have always been individuals

willing to carry that responsibility.

Men and women who believed the profession was worth protecting.

People who understood that the trust placed in them by their communities deserved to be honored with

care.

These individuals rarely sought recognition.

But their work shaped the reputation of the profession for everyone who followed.

The future of insurance will depend on whether the next generation chooses to follow their example.

Not perfectly.

But faithfully.

Because the strength of any profession ultimately rests not on its systems or its structures.

It rests on the character of the people who practice it.

And when those people choose integrity, the profession remains strong.

A Life Measured in Trust

One of the quiet truths about the insurance profession is that its real impact is rarely visible in a single

moment.

Unlike many professions where success can be measured immediately, the value of insurance often

reveals itself slowly, over years and sometimes over generations.

A policy written today may not be tested until long after the conversation that created it has been

forgotten.

Yet when that moment finally arrives, the outcome can shape the course of a family's life.

This is why the most respected professionals in the field often measure their careers not by annual

production numbers, but by something far more enduring.

They measure their work in trust.

Trust grows slowly.

It begins with small interactions.

A phone call returned promptly.

A question answered patiently.

An explanation offered without rushing through the details.

These moments may appear insignificant at the time, but over years they accumulate into something

powerful.

A reputation.

And reputation, once established, travels quietly through communities.

Consider how most people actually find their insurance advisor.

Rarely through advertising alone.

More often through a simple conversation.

A neighbor mentions the agent who helped them understand their coverage after a difficult storm.

A business owner recommends the advisor who took the time to review their risks carefully before

writing the policy.

A young family hears about the professional who helped their parents navigate a complicated claim.

These recommendations carry a kind of credibility that marketing can never fully replicate.

Because they come from experience.

Over time, the professional begins to see something remarkable happen.

The clients they once helped as young families begin to return years later with new needs.

The first home becomes a second home.

The small business expands into something larger.

The children who once sat quietly at the kitchen table during their parents' insurance conversation

eventually grow up and begin making their own decisions.

And when that moment arrives, many of them reach out to the same advisor their parents trusted.

This is how a career in insurance quietly becomes interwoven with the life of a community.

The professional witnesses milestones that extend far beyond the scope of the original policy.

They see the growth of businesses.

They see families weather difficult seasons and celebrate new beginnings.

They see entire neighborhoods change as new generations move into homes once occupied by older

ones.

Through it all, the advisor remains a steady presence.

There is something deeply meaningful about this kind of work.

Because it reminds the professional that their role is not limited to selling protection.

They are participating in the stability of the community itself.

When businesses survive unexpected hardships, employees keep their jobs.

When families recover after disasters, neighborhoods remain strong.

When individuals feel confident that their protection was arranged carefully, they move forward with a

greater sense of security.

In this way, the quiet decisions made in insurance offices ripple outward into the broader life of the

community.

The standard bearers of the profession understand this ripple effect.

They recognize that their advice carries consequences beyond the immediate transaction.

That recognition shapes the way they approach their work.

They take time to understand the full picture of a client's life.

They ask questions that help reveal risks others might overlook.

And they resist the temptation to rush through conversations that deserve patience.

Over decades, this approach produces something extraordinary.

A book of business that is built not merely on policies, but on relationships.

Each policy inside that book represents a story.

A family that trusted the advisor during an important moment.

A business owner who sought guidance while navigating uncertain risks.

A community member who recommended the professional because they believed others deserved the

same careful attention.

Seen this way, the book of business becomes something far more meaningful than a collection of

accounts.

It becomes a reflection of trust earned over time.

This kind of trust cannot be purchased.

It cannot be accelerated.

It grows only through consistent behavior repeated over many years.

Through honesty in moments when easier answers might have been more profitable.

Through patience when hurried transactions would have required less effort.

Through the quiet discipline of placing long-term relationships above short-term advantage.

The professionals who practice the work this way often discover something surprising.

Their careers become deeply fulfilling.

Not simply because they succeed financially, but because they recognize the positive influence their

work has had on the lives around them.

They see businesses that survived because risks were addressed early.

They see families who rebuilt after disasters because protection had been arranged properly.

They see communities that remained resilient because thoughtful advisors helped people prepare for

uncertainty.

These outcomes are rarely celebrated publicly.

But they represent the quiet victories of the profession.

And over time, those victories accumulate.

They form the legacy of the standard bearers.

Not a legacy measured only in numbers, but in the lives strengthened by the work they performed

faithfully.

For the next generation of professionals, these examples offer an important lesson.

Success in the insurance profession is not simply about selling policies.

It is about building trust that lasts long enough to shape the future of the people who depend on it.

The Culture of the Profession

Every profession carries an invisible culture.

It cannot be found in policy manuals or training materials.

It is not written into contracts or corporate mission statements.

Yet it exists everywhere the work is practiced.

It lives in the habits professionals develop. It appears in the tone of conversations between colleagues.

It shapes the way decisions are made when no one else is watching.

Culture determines what a profession truly values.

In insurance, culture has always been transmitted quietly.

Young agents rarely begin their careers with a full understanding of what the profession represents.

They learn by observation.

They watch how experienced professionals speak with clients.

They notice how mentors handle difficult conversations.

They observe whether decisions are guided by integrity or by convenience.

Over time, these examples become the unwritten curriculum of the profession.

A new agent might learn how to submit an application in a few hours.

They might learn how to quote a policy in a few days.

But learning how to practice the profession well takes much longer.

It requires watching people who have already developed judgment through experience.

The standard bearers serve this role.

They become the living examples that younger professionals imitate.

Consider how a new professional learns the importance of patience.

A mentor might sit beside them during a meeting with a client.

The conversation moves slowly.

The experienced advisor asks thoughtful questions rather than rushing toward a recommendation.

They listen carefully before offering guidance.

To an impatient observer, the conversation might seem inefficient.

But the young professional watching closely begins to understand something deeper.

Trust is being built.

And trust cannot be rushed.

Moments like these shape the culture of the profession more powerfully than any formal training program.

Because they demonstrate what the profession values in practice.

They show that listening matters.

They show that judgment matters.

They show that protecting a client's future is more important than completing a quick transaction.

Unfortunately, culture can also move in the opposite direction.

If young professionals enter offices where speed is valued above understanding, they quickly adopt

those habits.

If they observe conversations focused only on price, they assume that price is the most important

factor.

If they see shortcuts taken regularly, they begin to believe that shortcuts are acceptable.

Over time, these habits reshape the profession.

Not because anyone intentionally planned to change its values.

But because culture is always transmitted through example.

This is why the presence of standard bearers matters so much.

They stabilize the culture of the profession.

They demonstrate, through their behavior, what the work is supposed to represent.

They remind younger professionals that the purpose of the job is not simply to move policies through a

system.

It is to help people make thoughtful decisions about uncertain futures.

Many of the most influential figures in the profession never appear in industry publications.

They do not give keynote speeches.

They do not seek recognition.

Instead, they quietly mentor the people around them.

They answer questions patiently.

They explain mistakes openly so others can learn from them.

They encourage younger colleagues to slow down when important decisions are being made.

These mentors create a ripple effect that can last for decades.

A young professional who learns the profession from a person of integrity often carries those habits

throughout their entire career.

Years later, that same professional may become a mentor themselves.

They pass along the same lessons.

The same patience.

The same commitment to doing the work correctly even when it would be easier to cut corners.

This is how the profession renews itself.

Without this cycle of mentorship, the profession slowly loses its identity.

The technical knowledge might remain.

But the deeper understanding of responsibility begins to fade.

Policies may still be written.

But the spirit of the profession gradually disappears.

The standard bearers prevent this erosion.

They ensure that the profession remains grounded in the principles that originally gave it meaning.

When a young professional encounters one of these mentors early in their career, it often changes the

way they see the work forever.

They begin to realize that insurance is not merely about transactions.

It is about stewardship.

The steward protects something valuable on behalf of others.

They approach their responsibility with seriousness and care.

And they recognize that their actions influence people far beyond the immediate moment.

The culture of the profession ultimately depends on whether enough individuals choose to act as

stewards.

Each generation must decide what kind of example it will provide to the next.

If professionals demonstrate patience, integrity, and thoughtful judgment, those habits will continue.

If they demonstrate impatience and indifference, those habits will spread just as quickly.

Seen in this light, the work of the standard bearers extends far beyond their own careers.

They are shaping the character of the profession itself.

And through that influence, they help determine whether the profession will continue to serve

communities with the dignity it once possessed.

The Call to Carry the Profession

Every profession reaches moments when it must decide what it will become in the future.

Insurance now stands at such a moment.

The world is changing quickly. Technology continues to transform how businesses operate. Consumers

have access to more information than any generation before them.

Amid these changes, many people have questioned whether the traditional role of the insurance professional will continue to matter.

But the answer to that question does not lie in technology, systems, or market trends.

It lies in people.

The future of the profession will ultimately be shaped by the character of those who choose to practice

it.

Every generation inherits the profession from those who came before.

The previous generation built relationships, served communities, and carried the responsibility of

advising people through uncertain risks.

Now the responsibility passes forward.

The next generation must decide how they will carry it.

Some may treat the work as merely a transaction.

Policies may be written quickly.

Conversations may focus only on price.

Relationships may remain shallow and temporary.

If enough professionals choose that path, the profession will gradually lose the dignity that once defined

it.

But another path remains available.

The path taken by the standard bearers.

Professionals who understand that the work carries meaning beyond the transaction.

Individuals who approach their responsibilities with humility and seriousness.

Advisors who recognize that the decisions they guide today may shape the lives of their clients for

years to come.

Choosing this path requires patience.

It requires resisting the temptation to rush through conversations that deserve careful attention.

It requires the courage to recommend protection that serves the client's future rather than simply

satisfying the immediate desire for convenience.

And it requires integrity — the quiet discipline of doing what is right even when no one else is watching.

These qualities may not always produce immediate recognition.

But over time they produce something far more valuable.

Trust.

And trust, once earned, becomes the foundation upon which entire careers — and entire professions —

are built.

The encouraging truth is that every generation contains individuals willing to carry this responsibility.

People who believe the profession is worth preserving.

Professionals who see their work not simply as a job, but as a form of stewardship.

They understand that the promise contained within an insurance policy represents something deeply

human.

Protection.

Stability.

Peace of mind during uncertain moments.

When these professionals practice their work faithfully, communities notice.

Families feel safer knowing that someone knowledgeable and trustworthy is helping them navigate

difficult decisions.

Business owners move forward with confidence because they understand the protections supporting

their efforts.

And younger professionals entering the industry begin to see that the work offers something more

meaningful than they initially expected.

In this way, the standard bearers quietly renew the profession.

Not through dramatic changes or public announcements.

But through thousands of conversations handled with patience, honesty, and care.

Each conversation strengthens the trust between professional and client.

Each relationship strengthens the reputation of the profession itself.

And over time, these quiet acts of integrity accumulate into something powerful.

A profession that still deserves the trust placed in it.

The future of insurance will not be decided in a single moment.

It will be shaped gradually through the choices made by the people who practice the work each day.

Each recommendation offered with care.

Each conversation approached with patience.

Each decision guided by integrity.

These choices may seem small.

But across decades and communities, they define the character of the profession.

For those entering the industry today, the invitation is simple.

Carry the profession forward.

Honor the trust placed in you.

Learn from the mentors who practiced the work with dignity.

And become the kind of professional whose example will guide the next generation.

Because when enough individuals choose to practice the profession this way, something remarkable

happens.

The spirit that once defined insurance begins to reappear.

Clients once again see advisors rather than salespeople.

Communities rediscover the value of thoughtful guidance.

And the profession itself remembers what it was always meant to be.

Not merely an industry.

But a promise kept.

"Do what is right, not what is easy nor what is popular."

Roy T. Bennett

A Case Study From the Field

The Morning Everything Changed

There are moments in this profession where the work stops being theoretical.

No systems.

No metrics.

No production numbers.

Just names.

Real names.

Names you recognize.

November 5th, 2017 began like any other morning.

A quiet, cold Sunday across most of the country. Routine. Predictable. Unremarkable. The

kind of day that passes without notice. The kind of day no one expects to remember.

Until it isn't.

What happened in Sutherland Springs that morning would go on to change our county—and

our community—forever. But in the moment, it didn't arrive all at once. It came in fragments.

Headlines. Alerts. Messages that didn't quite make sense yet.

Like most people, I first became aware of it the same way everyone else did.

Through the news.

At first, it felt distant.

Tragic—but distant.

Another event happening somewhere else. Something you acknowledge, maybe reflect on

briefly, and then move forward with your day. That's how most people experience events like

that.

At least in the beginning.

That distance didn't last.

The following morning—Monday—I walked into the office at 7:45 a.m., fifteen minutes early

like I always did.

Routine has a way of grounding you.

Lights on. Coffee brewing. Computer starting up. The quiet rhythm of opening an office before

the day begins.

There was nothing unusual about the start of that day.

Nothing to suggest that within minutes, everything about it would change.

By 8:10 a.m., the tone had shifted.

The names started coming in.

At first, unofficial.

Then confirmed.

Lists began to circulate. Messages between people trying to verify what they were hearing.

Information moving faster than it could be fully understood.

And like agents do, we started checking.

Cross-referencing.

Looking for anything familiar.

Hoping not to find it.

But we did.

They weren't just names.

They were our clients.

As we continued cross-referencing, the full weight of it became clear.

Six of the individuals who lost their lives were connected to our agency.

Two more—also our clients—had been injured.

Eight families.

Eight households.

Eight relationships that, just days earlier, existed in the normal rhythm of everyday life.

The realization didn't arrive all at once.

It settled.

With each name.

The office didn't become loud.

It didn't become chaotic.

It became quiet.

Because there are moments where words don't help.

And this was one of them.

I remember the silence more than anything.

And I remember the names.

Two of those individuals were people I had been trying to sit down with.

We had talked about scheduling an annual review.

We had discussed life insurance.

They didn't have any in place.

Not because they didn't care.

Not because they didn't understand.

Because life gets in the way.

Schedules shift.

Priorities compete.

Meetings get pushed.

We had rescheduled more than once.

Each time with the assumption that there would be another opportunity.

Another conversation.

Another day.

There wasn't.

That realization doesn't leave you.

Not as blame.

But as weight.

There is a kind of clarity that only comes in moments like this.

Not intellectual clarity.

Not strategic clarity.

But moral clarity.

The understanding that this work is not built around convenience.

It is built around responsibility.

Responsibility that exists whether the timing fits—or not.

And in that moment, the work changed.

The First Response

Once the reality was clear, the question changed.

It was no longer about understanding what had happened.

It was about what needed to be done next.

There was no time to step back and process it fully.

No space to sit with it.

Because while we were still trying to make sense of the names—

Families were already living with the consequences.

In moments like that, the normal pace of the industry feels out of place.

Too slow.

Too structured.

Too far removed from what is actually happening.

The system does not stop.

It continues moving in its normal rhythm.

But the situation in front of you no longer fits that rhythm.

So the responsibility shifts.

Not away from the system—

But ahead of it.

The first call I made that morning was to our corporate office.

We needed to start the claims process immediately for the accidental death benefit tied to

their membership.

It wasn't large.

Five thousand dollars per person.

In the context of the loss, it was small.

But in the context of timing, it mattered.

Because the first response is not about solving the entire problem.

It is about creating stability in the middle of uncertainty.

Something immediate.

Something tangible.

Something that arrives before everything else is figured out.

That is what the earliest forms of protection were built around.

Not completeness.

Not precision.

Response.

And in moments like this, response carries more weight than structure.

We didn't need perfect information to act.

We didn't need every detail confirmed.

We needed to move.

The claims process was started.

Information was gathered.

What could be done immediately was done.

But even as that began, it was clear—

The system would not be enough on its own.

Not because it was broken.

Because it was built for something different.

It was built for consistency.

For scale.

For long-term resolution.

But what we were facing required something else.

Speed.

Presence.

Adaptability.

Things that don't always exist inside structured systems.

That realization didn't come as a criticism.

It came as clarity.

The system would respond.

But it would take time.

And time was the one thing these families did not have the luxury of waiting on.

That is where the role of the professional begins to change.

Not in title.

Not in responsibility as defined on paper.

But in posture.

You are no longer just facilitating a process.

You are standing in the gap between what has happened and what will eventually be

resolved.

That gap is not defined anywhere.

There are no guidelines for it.

No training modules.

No outlined expectations.

But it exists.

Every time.

And in that space, the work becomes something different.

It becomes personal.

Not because the system failed.

But because the system cannot be everything at once.

It cannot be immediate and exact at the same time.

It cannot be both deeply personal and broadly scalable without trade-offs.

And in moments like this, those trade-offs become visible.

The system begins to move.

But the need is already present.

So the question becomes:

What happens in between?

That is where people step in.

Not because they are instructed to.

Because they understand what is required.

The first response is rarely perfect.

It is rarely complete.

But it is necessary.

Because without it, the space between loss and resolution becomes too wide.

Too unstable.

Too uncertain.

And that uncertainty is what does the most damage in the early moments.

This is something the industry does not always talk about.

We focus on the structure.

The coverage.

The outcome.

But there is a period before all of that takes effect.

A period where people are waiting.

Trying to understand what happens next.

Trying to find something stable in the middle of something that has just been disrupted.

That is where the work begins.

Not when the claim is finalized.

Not when the system completes its process.

At the moment the need becomes real.

And in that moment, the professional has a choice.

To wait for the system to move.

Or to step forward and begin the work before it does.

That choice is not written anywhere.

It is not enforced.

It is not measured.

But it defines the difference between participation and responsibility.

Because responsibility does not begin when the system responds.

It begins when the need appears.

And once that is understood—

The way you approach the work changes.

When People Step Forward

By the time the initial response had begun, it was clear that what was
needed would extend

beyond anything the system could provide on its own.

The claims process was moving.

The first steps had been taken.

But there was still a gap.

Not in structure.

In timing.

The system would respond.

But it would take time to fully unfold.

And in that time, families were still trying to stabilize.

286

Still trying to understand what came next.

That is where the decision had to be made.

Not whether something should be done.

But who would take responsibility for doing it.

We received notice of an emergency meeting later that morning.

Two hours.

That was the window between understanding what had happened and deciding how we would

respond.

We sat down as an office.

Not as producers.

Not as individuals focused on performance.

But as people connected to what had just happened.

There was no structured plan waiting for us.

No directive from corporate.

No outlined solution.

Just a shared understanding:

We needed to act.

One of the other agents in the office had relationships with the remaining families.

He stepped forward immediately.

Volunteered to take the lead.

There was no hesitation.

No discussion about whether it made sense.

Just action.

That kind of response doesn't come from training.

It comes from posture.

And posture is formed long before moments like this arrive.

What we decided to do was simple.

We would host a drive-through barbecue plate sale.

Not as a business event.

Not as something tied to production or visibility.

But as a direct way to support the families affected.

Everything about it would be built around one principle:

Give what we can.

Give it quickly.

Give it directly.

There was no framework for it.

No system to plug into.

So we built it ourselves.

Our agency.

Our spouses.

Our children.

Everyone stepped in.

Not because they were asked.

Because they understood what was needed.

The timeline was short.

Three weeks.

Three weeks to plan it.

Organize it.

Promote it.

And execute it.

There were no guarantees.

No certainty around turnout.

No way to fully predict the outcome.

But that wasn't the focus.

The focus was movement.

We began reaching out.

Local businesses.

Suppliers.

Anyone willing to contribute.

Food was donated.

Supplies were donated.

Time was given freely.

What could have been complicated became simple.

Because no one was asking what they would gain.

They were asking how they could help.

Word spread.

Not through structured campaigns.

But through conversation.

Through people sharing it with one another.

And people showed up.

As the event came together, something else followed.

Attention.

News media reached out.

Cameras appeared.

And with them came individuals—some even at a national level— who wanted to be present.

On the surface, that kind of attention can feel validating.

It can create the sense that what is being done matters.

But in that moment, the question wasn't whether it mattered.

It was what it was for.

This was not an event built for recognition.

It was not designed to be publicized.

It was not created to elevate anyone involved in it.

It was built for one purpose:

To help people in need.

And that purpose had to be protected.

So we made a decision.

Those who came with cameras were asked to leave them behind.

Those who came looking for visibility were given a choice.

You can stay.

You can help.

You can serve alongside everyone else.

But the cameras stay in the car.

Or you can leave.

Because this was not an event for anyone's gain.

It was for the families.

That line mattered.

Not because attention is wrong.

But because attention changes posture.

It shifts focus.

It introduces incentive.

It creates the temptation to turn something meaningful into something visible.

And in moments like this, visibility was not the goal.

Presence was.

What followed was quiet.

The event moved forward without coverage.

No headlines.

No segments.

No cameras documenting what was happening.

And that was intentional.

Because the value of what was done was not measured in how many people saw it.

It was measured in how it was carried out.

On the day of the event, the line moved steadily.

Plate after plate.

Car after car.

We served approximately 2,000 plates.

Each one prepared, packaged, and handed out by people who had chosen to be there.

It wasn't polished.

It wasn't perfect.

But it worked.

Every dollar raised was given directly to the church.

To be distributed to the families affected.

No percentages taken.

No costs held back.

Just direct support.

This is what mutual aid looks like in practice.

Not theoretical.

Not historical.

Present.

It is not a replacement for the system.

It is what fills the gap when the system cannot move fast enough.

Because systems are designed for scale.

But scale creates distance.

And distance slows response.

Communities—and individuals willing to lead within them—do not have that distance.

They feel the impact.

They see the faces.

They know the names.

And proximity creates urgency.

There is a difference between contributing to something and taking responsibility for it.

Many are willing to support.

Fewer are willing to lead.

Leadership in moments like this is not about recognition.

It is about ownership.

Ownership of effort.

Ownership of coordination.

Ownership of follow-through.

And in moments like this, ownership cannot be assigned.

It has to be chosen.

What happened over those three weeks was not driven by obligation.

It was driven by that choice.

A choice to step forward instead of waiting.

A choice to act instead of observing.

A choice to carry responsibility when it would have been easier to assume someone else

would.

This is where the profession connects back to its origin.

Not in its structure.

Not in its systems.

But in its behavior.

Because before insurance became an industry—

It was people doing exactly this.

Seeing a need.

And responding to it directly.

Not because it was required.

Because it was understood.

The scale is different today.

The systems are more advanced.

The structure is more complex.

But moments like this reveal something simple:

The foundation has not changed.

When something breaks—

People still step forward.

And when they do—

The impact is immediate.

Not measured in policies.

Not tracked in reports.

But felt.

By the people who needed it most.

And remembered long after the moment has passed.

The Standard We Carry

What happened over those weeks was not complicated.

It was people stepping forward and doing what needed to be done.

No system required it.

No process dictated it.

It happened because someone chose to take responsibility.

And in doing so, it revealed something else.

Not just what we are capable of—

But how far we have drifted from carrying it consistently.

Because the truth is—

Most of the time, we operate as if there is always another opportunity.

Another meeting.

Another call.

Another chance to come back and finish what we didn't get to.

We tell ourselves we'll follow up next week.

We tell ourselves we'll circle back when things slow down.

We tell ourselves the conversation can wait.

And most of the time—

It can.

Until it can't.

That is the part of this profession that does not get talked about enough.

The gap between knowing something matters…

And acting like it does.

Every agent understands risk.

Every agent knows the importance of protection.

Every agent has had the conversation about life insurance, liability, or coverage gaps.

That is not the issue.

The issue is urgency.

Because knowledge without urgency becomes delay.

And delay, over time, becomes exposure.

Not intentional.

Not reckless.

Just postponed.

Two of the individuals connected to this event were people I had intended to meet with.

We had talked about sitting down.

We had talked about reviewing their coverage.

We had talked about life insurance.

And it didn't happen.

Not because they said no.

Because it kept getting moved.

That is where the standard is either upheld—

Or quietly lowered.

Not in the big decisions.

In the small ones.

In whether you press just a little harder to get the meeting scheduled.

In whether you let it slide when it becomes inconvenient.

In whether you accept "later" as an answer—without understanding what later actually risks.

Because later is not guaranteed.

This profession is built around events that have not happened yet.

Which makes it easy to treat everything as if there is still time.

But the reality is—

The work only matters if it is done before it is needed.

After that, it is too late to change it.

That is where the emotional weight of this work comes from.

Not in selling a policy.

Not in structuring coverage.

But in understanding that what is being discussed carries consequences.

And that responsibility is not just technical.

It is human.

It is tied to families.

To outcomes.

To moments that do not give you the chance to go back and adjust what was missed.

That is what this profession was built to carry.

Not just information.

Not just transactions.

Responsibility.

But over time, that responsibility has been softened.

Not removed.

Just pushed behind process.

Behind speed.

Behind the pressure to move on to the next thing.

Because slowing down is uncomfortable.

Pressing into a conversation takes effort.

Holding the line when something matters takes time.

And time is the one thing most people feel like they don't have.

But moments like this force a different perspective.

Because in those moments—

Time is the only thing that mattered.

Not how efficient the process was.

Not how quickly something could be quoted.

But whether the right decisions had already been made.

That is where this profession is either practiced at a high level—

Or reduced to a transaction.

Because transactions move quickly.

Responsibility does not.

Responsibility slows down.

Responsibility asks more questions.

Responsibility stays in the conversation longer than is comfortable.

Not to make the sale.

But to make sure the outcome is right.

That is the difference.

And it is not something that can be automated.

It is not something that can be delegated to a system.

It is something that has to be carried.

Intentionally.

Consistently.

Especially in the moments where it would be easier not to.

Because the standard is not what we say we believe.

It is what we carry when there is still time to act.

And if that standard is not carried consistently—

Then moments like this will continue to expose it.

The Work We Were Meant to Carry

What happened in those weeks was not new.

It only felt that way.

Because over time, the profession has moved so far toward structure, process, and scale—

That when something simple shows up again, it feels different.

But it isn't.

It is a return.

A return to what this work was always meant to be.

Long before policies were standardized…

Before systems were built…

Before the profession became what it is today—

There were people who understood something fundamental.

When a family suffers loss—

The response cannot wait.

Not for approval.

Not for process.

Not for the system to catch up.

That belief is not modern.

It is foundational.

Michael J. McGivney built his work around that exact principle.

Not as a business model.

Not as a strategy.

But as a responsibility.

To widows.

To children.

To families who suddenly found themselves without stability

He did not create something complex.

He created something immediate.

A structure where people came together to support one another when something went wrong.

Not eventually.

Not after everything had been reviewed.

But in the moment it was needed.

That is where this profession began.

Not in contracts.

Not in underwriting.

In mutual aid.

People stepping forward.

Taking responsibility.

Carrying one another through moments they could not carry alone.

What happened in this case study is no different.

It is not innovation.

It is not a new model.

It is a reflection.

A reflection of what still exists beneath everything that has been built on top of it.

Because even now—

When something breaks—

People still step in.

They still give their time.

They still give their resources.

They still take responsibility when there is no system requiring them to.

The difference is—

We no longer expect it.

We treat it as something exceptional.

But it was never meant to be exceptional.

It was meant to be the standard.

The system was built to support that standard.

Not replace it.

But over time, that relationship has shifted.

The system has become the focus.

And the responsibility has been pushed to the background.

Not intentionally.

Gradually.

Through efficiency.

Through scale.

Through the pressure to move faster.

And in that shift, something important has been lost.

Not the ability to respond.

The expectation to.

Moments like this bring that back into focus.

They remind us that the profession is not defined by what it promises on paper.

It is defined by how it shows up when those promises are tested.

And when that moment comes—

The system will respond.

But the person will be remembered.

For whether they stepped forward.

Or whether they waited.

That is the work.

Not just writing policies.

Not just structuring coverage.

Carrying responsibility.

Before the moment.

During the moment.

After the moment.

That is what this profession was built on.

And that is what it still requires.

Not more systems.

Not more speed.

More ownership.

Because in the end—

The strength of the profession is not measured by how efficient it becomes.

It is measured by whether it still holds onto the reason it was created in the first place.

And that reason has never changed.

When something goes wrong—

People need someone to step forward.

Not later.

Now.

"The Price of Greatness is Responsibility"

Winston Churchill

Another Case Study From the Field: The Conversation That Didn't Land

Not every failure in this profession happens because something was missed.

Some happen because something was explained—

And not accepted.

A client I inherited through a transfer into our agency—Mr. Smith—called and said he wanted

to come in and lower his insurance.

That was the request.

Not a review.

Not a conversation.

A result.

I told him to come in the next morning.

We set the appointment for 10:00 a.m.

Not to make a change.

To go through his coverage properly.

He arrived late.

Around 10:45.

And from the moment he sat down, it was clear—

He still wasn't there for a review.

He wanted to lower his rates.

Move quickly.

Be done.

I stopped him there.

Because that's not how I operate.

There is a process.

Not because the system requires it—

Because responsibility does.

I had already prepared.

Pulled his account.

Reviewed his policies.

Prefilled my review form so we could walk through everything clearly and efficiently.

And that's what we did.

Line by line.

Auto coverage first.

He was carrying 50/100/50 limits.

No uninsured motorist coverage.

Five hundred dollar deductibles on comprehensive and collision.

And as I reviewed his loss history—

There was a pattern.

An accident every two to three years.

Not extreme.

But consistent.

The kind of pattern that matters.

I walked him through it.

What the limits meant.

What they didn't protect.

Where the exposure existed.

I explained how his current structure didn't align with his situation.

He drove a four-year-old Chevy High Country Tahoe.

Value mattered.

Usage mattered.

History mattered.

And none of those supported reducing coverage.

He became impatient.

Not because the process was unclear—

Because it wasn't fast enough.

"Just tell me what the cheapest option is."

But that's not what we were there to do.

He had come in for a result.

I made it a conversation.

And I stayed in it.

That's when he told me what had changed.

He had received a bonus.

Paid off the vehicle.

And now—

He wanted the cheapest option available.

I told him exactly what that meant.

State minimum liability.

No comprehensive.

No collision.

No uninsured motorist.

I told him I did not recommend it.

Not for his situation.

Not with his history.

Not with the asset he was driving.

He understood.

He just didn't agree.

He made it clear.

He was the client.

And he wanted the change made.

So I documented everything.

The review.

The recommendations.

The gaps.

The request.

And I had him sign.

Not as a formality.

As acknowledgment.

That he understood exactly what he was choosing.

The change was processed.

He saved roughly seven hundred and fifty dollars over six months.

He was satisfied.

And he left.

The Call That Changed the Conversation

It was a Saturday night.

Around 8:30.

Not a time most people expect to hear from a client.

But in this profession, those are usually the calls that matter most.

My phone rang.

It was Mr. Smith.

His tone was different.

Gone was the impatience.

Gone was the urgency to move quickly.

What replaced it was something else.

Panic.

He told me he was in Houston.

At a concert.

He had just been in an accident.

He said he wasn't paying attention.

Looked down for a moment.

And then it happened.

He T-boned another vehicle.

A newer Mercedes SUV.

Still carrying paper plates.

The kind of accident that doesn't leave much room for minor damage.

His Tahoe was heavily damaged.

From the way he described it—

Likely totaled.

But that wasn't what he was focused on.

His first question wasn't about fault.

Or injuries.

It was about the process.

"What do I do?"

So I walked him through it.

Gave him the claims number.

Explained the next steps.

The things you say in that moment to bring structure back into a situation that suddenly feels

out of control.

And then he asked the question.

"How fast will the adjuster cut me a check for my new car?"

There was a pause.

Not because I didn't understand what he was asking.

But because I understood exactly what he didn't.

So I asked him a question in return.

"What do you mean?"

He repeated it.

About the check.

About replacing the vehicle.

That's when the reality of the earlier conversation came back into the room.

Not as a memory.

As a consequence.

I explained it to him.

Slowly.

Clearly.

The same way I had just weeks before.

"You don't have coverage on your vehicle."

No comprehensive.

No collision.

There is no check coming for your Tahoe.

There was silence on the other end.

Not confusion.

Recognition.

Then I continued.

"The limits you selected—state minimum liability—"

"Thirty thousand per person."

"Sixty thousand total for bodily injury."

"Twenty-five thousand for property damage."

Another pause.

Longer this time.

Because now the situation was becoming clearer.

Not just what had happened—

But what it meant.

The vehicle he hit.

The damage it likely sustained.

The exposure that now existed.

And the gap between what was covered—

And what wasn't.

He said it quietly.

"I just wanted to save some money."

There was no frustration in his voice now.

No urgency.

Just realization.

And in that moment—

There was nothing left to adjust.

The policy was correct.

It matched exactly what he had requested.

The system had done its job.

But the outcome—

Was something else entirely.

The Cost of the Decision

There is a difference between understanding something—

And experiencing it.

Up until that moment, everything we had discussed was theoretical.

Coverage.

Limits.

Exposure.

All of it existed as information.

Now it didn't.

Now it was real.

A damaged vehicle.

Another driver involved.

A situation that would not resolve itself with time.

The Tahoe he had been driving—

The one he had just paid off—

Was no longer an asset.

It was a loss.

And there was no coverage in place to respond to it.

No comprehensive.

No collision.

Which meant there was no path for recovery through the policy.

The cost of that decision was now his to carry.

Fully.

And then there was the other side of the accident.

The vehicle he struck.

A newer Mercedes SUV.

Not a minor repair.

Not a simple claim.

The kind of loss that moves quickly beyond basic limits.

And that's where the structure of the policy began to matter.

Not in theory.

In reality.

State minimum liability.

Thirty thousand per person.

Sixty thousand total for bodily injury.

Twenty-five thousand for property damage.

Numbers that feel sufficient—

Until they are tested.

Because when the damage exceeds those limits—

The policy doesn't stretch.

It stops.

And whatever remains—

Doesn't disappear.

It transfers.

To the person responsible.

And at that point—

The situation changes.

Because once the limits of a policy are exceeded—

The protection the policy provides begins to fall away.

The claim no longer exists strictly within the structure of the policy.

It moves beyond it.

And when that happens—

The other party is no longer limited to what the policy will pay.

They can pursue recovery beyond those limits.

Through the legal system.

At that stage—

It is no longer about coverage.

It becomes a matter of liability.

And whatever is determined—

Is no longer defined by the policy that was selected.

But by the outcome of that process.

That is the part most people don't fully consider.

Not because they don't hear it.

Because they haven't felt it.

Until that moment.

And once it becomes real—

There is no adjustment.

No opportunity to revisit the decision.

No chance to restructure the coverage.

No way to go back and fill the gap that was left open.

The policy was written correctly.

It reflected exactly what had been requested.

But it was never designed to handle what actually happened.

And that difference—

Between what is written and what is needed—

Is where the real cost shows up.

Not in the premium that was saved.

But in the exposure that was created.

Seven hundred and fifty dollars in savings.

In exchange for tens of thousands—

Potentially more—

In responsibility.

Not spread out.

Not absorbed.

Carried.

Directly.

There is no system that offsets that.

No process that reduces it after the fact.

Because the system only responds to what exists.

And in this case—

The structure that existed was limited.

By choice.

That is the part that makes this difficult.

Not that something unexpected happened.

But that the outcome followed exactly what had been set in motion.

Nothing malfunctioned.

Nothing was missed.

Everything worked the way it was designed to.

And still—

The result was heavy.

That is where the difference becomes clear.

Between a transaction—

And a responsibility.

Because a transaction focuses on the moment.

The price.

The change.

The immediate result.

Responsibility looks further.

At what happens if something goes wrong.

At what the decision actually carries with it.

And whether the structure in place can hold up when it is tested.

In this case—

It couldn't.

Not because the system failed.

But because the standard was not carried all the way through.

And once the moment arrived—

That difference became permanent.

The Standard Does Not Change

There is a natural instinct in moments like this—

To assign blame.

To look back at the decision.

To revisit the conversation.

To question how it could have gone differently.

But this profession is not built on hindsight.

It is built on responsibility in the moment.

And in this case—

The moment was handled correctly.

The conversation happened.

The review was completed.

The risks were explained.

The gaps were made clear.

The recommendation was given.

And the decision—

Was still made.

That is where the role of the professional has to be understood clearly.

Because the responsibility is not to control the outcome.

It is to guide it.

To slow the conversation down.

To ask the right questions.

To explain what matters—

Even when it is not what the client wants to hear.

That is the work.

Not just processing a request.

But holding a standard.

Even when it creates tension.

Even when it takes more time.

Even when the client is pushing for speed.

Because the easy path is always available.

Quote it.

Change it.

Move on.

And in the moment—

That feels efficient.

But efficiency is not the measure of this profession.

Outcome is.

And outcomes are shaped long before the moment they are tested.

That is why the standard cannot shift.

Not based on the client.

Not based on the situation.

Not based on how busy the day is.

Because once the standard becomes flexible—

The result becomes unpredictable.

In this case, the standard was held.

The conversation did not get rushed.

The recommendation did not get softened.

The risk was not ignored.

And that matters.

Because the role of the professional is not to force a decision—

But to make sure the decision is understood.

Completely.

Clearly.

Without assumption.

That line is important.

Because there is a difference between influence—

And control.

A professional can influence.

Through knowledge.

Through experience.

Through clarity.

But control belongs to the client.

And that is where the outcome ultimately lives.

Not in what was said.

But in what was accepted.

That is why documentation matters.

Not as protection for the agent.

But as a reflection of the process.

That the conversation happened.

That the recommendation was made.

That the decision was acknowledged.

Because once the moment passes—

That is all that remains.

The process.

And whether it was carried with integrity.

This is where the profession often gets misunderstood.

When something goes wrong—

People look for a failure in execution.

But sometimes—

There isn't one.

Sometimes the process is followed exactly as it should be.

And the outcome still carries weight.

That does not mean the standard failed.

It means the standard was not accepted.

And that distinction matters.

Because lowering the standard to match the decision—

Does not improve the outcome.

It only removes the clarity.

The role of the professional is not to make every outcome perfect.

It is to make every conversation honest.

To make every recommendation grounded.

And to make every decision understood for what it truly is.

Because when that happens—

Even if the decision is not the right one—

It is still an informed one.

And that is where the responsibility shifts.

Not away from the professional—

But to the person making the choice.

That is the line this profession operates on.

And it is one that cannot be blurred.

Not for convenience.

Not for speed.

Not for the sake of keeping a client comfortable.

Because comfort in the moment—

Often creates consequences later.

And those consequences do not recognize intention.

Only structure.

Only decision.

Only what was put in place before the moment arrived.

That is why the standard does not change.

Because the moment eventually does.

What Happens When It's Not Accepted

What happened in this situation is not rare.

It is not extreme.

It is not something that only shows up in unusual circumstances.

It happens every day.

Quietly.

In conversations where someone is trying to move quickly.

In decisions where the focus shifts from responsibility—

To convenience.

There was no large-scale tragedy here like the one before.

No moment that brought a community together.

Just a conversation.

A process.

And a decision.

And in this case—

The process was carried fully.

The review was completed.

The risks were explained.

The gaps were made clear.

The recommendation was given—

Directly.

Nothing was skipped.

Nothing was softened.

Nothing was left unclear.

That matters.

Because the role of the professional is not to control the outcome—

It is to make sure the outcome is understood before it arrives.

In this case—

That standard was upheld.

But understanding alone is not enough.

Because mutual aid does not exist in explanation.

It exists in acceptance.

And that is where the difference shows up.

Not in what was said—

But in what was chosen.

In the earlier case—

Responsibility was carried fully.

People stepped forward.

Not because they had to—

Because they understood what was required.

And because of that—

Something was built.

Support.

Relief.

A system that responded when it was needed most.

This case is different.

Not because the process failed.

But because the decision did not follow the standard that was presented.

And once that happens—

The structure that is put in place can only do so much.

That is the part of this profession that often goes unspoken.

The outcome is not determined only by the professional.

It is shared.

Between guidance—

And acceptance.

Between what is recommended—

And what is chosen.

Mutual aid depends on both.

It cannot exist fully without alignment between them.

That was the foundation of this profession.

Long before systems.

Long before scale.

Michael J. McGivney understood that clearly.

The work was not about transactions.

It was about people taking responsibility—

For themselves.

And for one another.

Not eventually.

Immediately.

And that kind of system only works—

When responsibility is not only explained—

But accepted.

Because when it is not—

The system still functions.

But the outcome changes.

Not because something broke.

But because something was declined.

That is the difference.

And that difference—

Even when it seems small in the moment—

Becomes significant when it is tested.

The standard was there.

The process was followed.

The decision was made.

And when the moment arrived—

Everything responded exactly as it had been set.

That is the weight of this profession.

Not just in what is offered—

But in what is chosen.

Because when something goes wrong—

That is all that remains.

"We are what we repeatedly do. Excellence, then, is not an act but a habit."

Aristotle

FINAL REFLECTION: Carrying the Promise Forward

Remembering Where It Began

Every profession begins with a need.

Not a market opportunity. Not a business model.

A need.

Insurance began the same way.

Long before policies were printed or companies were formed, communities faced a simple and painful

reality: life is uncertain, and when misfortune strikes, it rarely affects only one person.

A fire that destroys a home does not merely remove a structure.

It disrupts a family.

An accident that injures a worker does not only affect that individual.

It affects the household that depends upon them.

A failed harvest, a damaged shop, or the loss of a breadwinner can ripple outward until entire families

find themselves standing on the edge of ruin.

For much of human history, there were few institutions capable of absorbing these shocks.

And so communities did what communities have always done.

They relied on one another.

Neighbors helped rebuild homes.

Churches organized support for struggling families.

Local associations gathered funds so widows and children would not be left completely alone when

tragedy arrived.

This instinct — the instinct to protect one another from the harshest consequences of misfortune — is the moral foundation from which the insurance profession eventually emerged.

At its heart, insurance was never merely about contracts.

It was about solidarity.

Over time, this instinct became organized.

Communities began forming mutual aid societies.

Members contributed small amounts regularly so that when tragedy struck one member of the group,

the collective resources could provide relief.

It was not a perfect system.

But it represented something profoundly human.

A recognition that no individual should face life's uncertainties entirely alone.

These early efforts laid the groundwork for what would eventually become the modern insurance

industry.

Yet as the profession evolved and grew more sophisticated, the memory of those humble beginnings

sometimes faded.

Policies became more complex.

Organizations became larger.

Processes became more technical.

None of these developments were inherently wrong.

In many ways they improved the ability of insurance institutions to provide reliable protection at scale.

But as the systems grew larger, the profession occasionally drifted away from the simple human

impulse that gave birth to it.

The impulse to care for one another in times of uncertainty.

In the nineteenth century, one man would help remind the profession — and the communities around

him — of that original spirit.

His name was Father Michael J. McGivney.

Father McGivney lived in a time when working families often faced devastating financial hardship after

the death of a wage earner.

A father who died unexpectedly could leave behind a widow with several children and no reliable

means of support.

Many widows were forced to rely on charity.

Some families were separated as children were sent to orphanages because their mothers could not

provide for them alone.

These tragedies were not rare.

They were painfully common.

And Father McGivney saw them firsthand as he served the families in his parish.

He understood something important.

The suffering these families faced was not caused by a lack of love within the community.

People cared deeply about their neighbors.

But goodwill alone could not overcome economic reality.

Families needed a system that allowed them to protect one another in a structured and reliable way.

So Father McGivney helped create one.

In 1882, he founded what would become the Knights of Columbus.

At its core, the organization was a mutual aid society.

Members contributed to a shared fund that would support families when tragedy struck.

If a member died, the organization helped ensure that his widow and children would not be abandoned

to financial ruin.

It was a simple idea.

But it carried extraordinary moral weight.

Because it transformed compassion into action.

Father McGivney did not see this effort as merely financial.

He saw it as an expression of community responsibility.

The members of the organization were not simply purchasing protection.

They were standing beside one another.

They were affirming a principle that remains just as important today as it was then:

No family should face the hardships of life completely alone.

The modern insurance profession, in many ways, is an extension of that same idea.

The systems may be larger. The policies more detailed. The companies more complex.

But beneath those structures lies the same principle.

Protection shared across a community.

Risk carried together rather than alone.

Remembering this origin changes the way one sees the profession.

Insurance stops being merely a financial product.

It becomes part of a much larger human story.

A story about responsibility. About solidarity. About the quiet determination of communities to protect

one another from the harshest consequences of life's uncertainty.

When professionals remember this story, their work begins to take on deeper meaning.

They are not merely facilitating transactions.

They are participating in a tradition that stretches back through generations.

A tradition rooted in the belief that people should stand beside one another when life becomes difficult.

And that belief — more than any system or policy structure — is the true heart of the insurance

Profession.

The Quiet Work of Father McGivney

To understand why Father Michael J. McGivney's example continues to resonate more than a century

later, one must first understand the world in which he lived.

The late nineteenth century was a difficult time for many immigrant families in the United States.

Industrialization was expanding rapidly. Cities were growing. Opportunity existed, but so did hardship.

Many immigrant men worked dangerous jobs in factories, railroads, and construction. Safety

regulations were limited, wages were modest, and the loss of a single paycheck could send an entire

household into crisis.

When a working father died, the consequences were often devastating.

Widows frequently had few employment opportunities available to them. Many families had no savings.

Without assistance, mothers faced the impossible decision of trying to support their children alone or

placing them into orphanages where they might receive food and shelter.

These situations were not rare exceptions.

They were tragically common.

And Father McGivney encountered them regularly in the parish he served in New Haven, Connecticut.

McGivney was not a man of wealth or political power.

He did not command great institutions or vast resources.

What he possessed instead was something far more important.

He possessed a deep sense of pastoral responsibility for the families entrusted to his care.

As a parish priest, he baptized children, celebrated marriages, and comforted families in times of loss.

He saw the full arc of human life unfold within his community.

And through those experiences, he began to see a pattern.

The suffering faced by widows and children after the death of a father was not simply a matter of

personal tragedy.

It was a systemic problem.

The community lacked a reliable structure to protect families when their primary provider was suddenly

gone.

McGivney believed the solution required something more than charity.

Charity could help temporarily, but it could not create stability.

What families needed was a system of mutual responsibility.

A way for men within the community to stand beside one another and ensure that no family would face

catastrophe alone.

This idea was both practical and deeply moral.

Each member of the community would contribute modestly to a shared fund.

If tragedy struck one member, the community would respond collectively.

In this way, the burden of misfortune would be distributed across many shoulders rather than crushing

a single family.

When McGivney founded the Knights of Columbus in 1882, he was not attempting to build a corporate

institution.

He was creating a brotherhood rooted in faith, charity, and mutual aid.

Members pledged to support one another.

And importantly, they pledged to protect the families left behind if one of their brothers died.

In doing so, McGivney created something remarkable.

He transformed the instinct of compassion into an organized system of protection.

The idea was simple.

But its impact was profound.

What makes McGivney's story especially powerful is the humility with which he carried out his work.

He did not seek recognition.

He did not pursue fame.

His goal was simply to serve the families around him.

History often celebrates individuals who command great attention or achieve visible success.

Yet many of the people who shape communities most profoundly do so quietly.

They lead through service rather than ambition.

They build structures that outlast them.

And they focus their energy not on personal recognition but on the well-being of others.

Father McGivney belonged firmly in this category.

His life was not long.

He died in 1890 at the age of only thirty-eight.

His passing came after years of tireless work serving his parish and supporting the organization he had

helped create.

Although he could not have known it at the time, the institution he founded would continue to grow and

serve millions of families across generations.

Today the Knights of Columbus is one of the largest fraternal organizations in the world.

Yet the true significance of McGivney's legacy cannot be measured only by numbers.

Its deeper significance lies in the principle that inspired it.

A principle that still speaks directly to the modern insurance profession.

That principle is simple:

Protection is an expression of love for one's community.

When individuals come together to share risk and support one another during hardship, they affirm

something fundamental about human dignity.

They affirm that no person should be abandoned in their most vulnerable moments.

In many ways, the insurance profession now carries forward the very idea McGivney helped put into

action.

Modern insurance institutions may operate on a larger scale.

But the principle remains the same.

Many people contribute small amounts into a shared system.

When tragedy strikes one member of that system, the collective resources respond.

The loss of one becomes manageable because it is shared by many.

Seen in this light, the work of the insurance professional takes on deeper meaning.

It is not merely administrative.

It is not merely financial.

It is part of a tradition rooted in mutual responsibility.

A tradition that recognizes the fragility of life and seeks to protect people from its harshest

consequences.

Father McGivney likely never imagined that his efforts would one day be connected to an entire

industry.

Yet the moral impulse behind his work continues to echo through the profession.

Every time a family receives the protection they need.

Every time a widow is able to maintain her home after the loss of a spouse.

Every time a business survives a disaster because proper coverage was in place.

The spirit of mutual aid that McGivney championed is present once again.

Remembering this history matters.

Because professions sometimes lose sight of the values that originally shaped them.

Processes become more important than purpose.

Efficiency replaces empathy.

Transactions overshadow relationships.

When this happens, the profession may continue to function, but it begins to lose its soul.

The story of Father McGivney reminds us that the true purpose of protection has always been human.

It exists to support families.

To stabilize communities.

And to ensure that when life's inevitable hardships arrive, individuals are not left to face them alone.

For modern professionals, remembering this heritage can change the way the work is approached.

It encourages patience when advising clients.

It encourages humility when making recommendations.

And it reinforces the idea that the profession carries responsibilities that extend far beyond individual

transactions.

In the quiet example of Father McGivney, we find a reminder of what the profession can be at its best.

Not merely a system of policies and premiums.

But a community standing together in the face of uncertainty.

The Profession at the Crossroads

Every generation eventually faces a moment when it must decide what kind of profession it will leave

behind.

Insurance now stands at such a moment.

The world surrounding the industry is changing rapidly. Technology has altered how information moves.

Automation has simplified many administrative processes. Clients have access to more tools and

resources than ever before.

In many ways, these developments are positive.

Efficiency can improve service. Technology can reduce errors. Systems can help professionals focus

their time where it matters most.

But alongside these improvements, another quieter trend has unfolded within the profession.

Something essential has slowly begun to fade.

For much of its history, insurance was practiced as a deeply relational profession.

Agents knew the families they served.

They understood the businesses operating in their communities.

They sat across kitchen tables and listened carefully as people described their hopes, their fears, and

the responsibilities they carried for those who depended upon them.

In those conversations, the professional's role was not simply to present options.

It was to guide judgment.

Clients relied on the professional's experience to help them understand risks they might never have

considered on their own.

This relationship created trust.

And trust created stability.

Yet over time, the industry began shifting toward a different rhythm.

Growth strategies emphasized scale.

Processes emphasized speed.

Systems emphasized efficiency.

None of these changes were entirely wrong.

But when efficiency becomes the dominant value of a profession, something subtle begins to happen.

The deeper purpose of the work becomes harder to see.

Professionals begin to think primarily in terms of transactions rather than stewardship.

Clients begin to feel like accounts rather than relationships.

The profession continues to function, but its spirit becomes diluted.

Many experienced professionals have sensed this shift.

They have seen how quickly the industry can move when convenience becomes the primary objective.

Applications are completed faster.

Policies are issued more quickly.

Interactions are shorter and more transactional.

From a purely operational perspective, these developments appear efficient.

Yet efficiency alone does not define a profession.

A profession exists to serve people.

And people rarely fit neatly into efficient systems.

Their lives are complex.

Their risks are unpredictable.

Their needs change over time.

The role of the professional has always been to navigate this complexity with care.

To ask thoughtful questions.

To slow down conversations when important decisions are being made.

To help clients understand not only what they can afford today, but what protections may matter years

from now.

These conversations require patience.

They require experience.

And they require a sense of responsibility that cannot be automated.

This is where the example of Father Michael J. McGivney becomes particularly relevant to the modern

profession.

McGivney did not build a system focused on efficiency alone.

He built a community grounded in responsibility.

Members understood that they were protecting one another.

The system existed not for convenience, but for stability.

Its purpose was to ensure that when tragedy arrived, families would not face it alone.

Modern insurance operates on a much larger scale, but the moral principle remains identical.

The profession exists to help individuals and families navigate uncertainty.

And uncertainty, by its nature, requires judgment.

No algorithm can fully understand the nuances of a family's situation.

No automated system can completely replace the wisdom gained through years of real-world

experience.

Technology may assist the professional.

But it cannot replace the human responsibility that lies at the center of the work.

This realization places the profession at a crossroads.

One path leads toward increasing automation and transactional efficiency.

On that path, professionals gradually become intermediaries between systems and clients.

Their role becomes narrower.

Their influence becomes smaller.

The work becomes easier to perform but less meaningful to practice.

The other path leads back toward stewardship.

On this path, professionals embrace technology as a tool while preserving the relational core of the

profession.

They use systems to reduce administrative burdens so they can spend more time understanding the

lives of the people they serve.

They remember that their greatest value lies not in processing applications, but in guiding judgment.

And they approach their responsibilities with the same seriousness that earlier generations carried

when the profession was still young.

Choosing this path requires intention.

It requires professionals who are willing to slow down when the world around them insists on speed.

It requires mentors who pass down not only technical knowledge but ethical standards.

And it requires individuals who recognize that their reputation is built not on the number of policies they

write, but on the trust they earn over time.

The encouraging truth is that such professionals still exist in every corner of the industry.

They may not always appear in headlines.

They may not speak on conference stages.

But they quietly serve families year after year, building relationships that span generations.

These individuals carry forward the tradition that figures like Father McGivney helped establish.

They understand that the profession's true purpose has never been purely financial.

It has always been human.

When enough professionals choose this path, the spirit of the profession begins to reappear.

Clients rediscover the value of trusted advisors.

Communities once again see insurance professionals as guides rather than vendors.

And the work regains the dignity that first attracted many people to the profession in the beginning.

The future of insurance will not be determined by technology alone.

It will be determined by the character of the people who choose to practice it.

Each generation must decide what values it will carry forward.

And in that decision lies the true destiny of the profession.

The Standard We Carry

Every profession ultimately lives or dies by the character of the people who practice it.

Systems may evolve.

Technology may improve.

Organizations may grow larger and more complex.

But none of these forces determine the true character of a profession.

That character is shaped by individuals.

By the choices they make when guiding clients.

By the integrity they carry into their work each day.

By the quiet standards they hold themselves to when no one else is watching.

The insurance profession has always depended on this kind of character.

Because at its core, the profession deals with uncertainty.

Families cannot predict when illness may strike.

Businesses cannot foresee every disaster that might interrupt their work.

Communities cannot avoid every storm, accident, or unexpected loss.

The professional's role has always been to help people prepare for the unknown.

That responsibility cannot be fulfilled through systems alone.

It requires judgment.

It requires experience.

And above all, it requires trust.

Trust is not created through advertising.

It is not built through marketing campaigns or corporate slogans.

Trust is built slowly.

It grows through honest conversations.

Through thoughtful recommendations.

Through the steady demonstration that the professional's first concern is the well-being of the client

rather than the convenience of the transaction.

Over time, these small actions accumulate.

And eventually a reputation begins to form.

Clients come to see the professional not merely as someone who sells policies.

But as someone they can rely upon when life becomes uncertain.

This reputation is the true legacy of the profession.

Policies may expire.

Companies may merge.

Technologies may change.

But the trust built between a professional and the people they serve can endure for generations.

Families remember the advisor who helped their parents protect their home.

Business owners remember the professional who guided them through their first difficult claim.

Young professionals remember the mentor who taught them how to practice the work with integrity.

These memories form the living culture of the profession.

When we reflect on the example of Father Michael J. McGivney, we see that the same principle guided

his life.

He did not create the Knights of Columbus as a business venture.

He created it as an expression of responsibility toward the families in his community.

He recognized that protection was not merely financial.

It was moral.

It was communal.

And it was deeply human.

The modern insurance professional carries forward that same responsibility, whether they realize it or

not.

Every conversation with a client represents a moment when the profession's reputation is either

strengthened or weakened.

Every recommendation offered with care reinforces the trust that generations before have built.

And every act of integrity reminds the community that the profession still exists to serve people rather

than systems.

This realization should not feel like a burden.

It should feel like a calling.

Because few professions have the opportunity to influence lives in such meaningful ways.

When practiced well, insurance stabilizes families.

It preserves businesses.

It helps communities recover after events that might otherwise destroy them.

These outcomes are not abstract.

They are deeply personal.

And the professionals who help make them possible become part of the story of the communities they

serve.

For those entering the profession today, the invitation is simple.

Carry the profession forward.

Learn the technical skills necessary to perform the work well.

But do not stop there.

Learn the deeper lessons that cannot be found in manuals or training courses.

Learn patience.

Learn humility.

Learn how to listen carefully when clients speak about their responsibilities and fears.

And most importantly, learn to treat the promise contained within every policy as something sacred.

The future of the profession will not be determined by the speed of its systems.

It will be determined by the standards of the people who represent it.

Every generation has the opportunity to elevate those standards.

To restore the dignity of the work.

To demonstrate once again that insurance is not merely a product.

It is a promise.

And perhaps that is the most fitting way to remember the legacy of Father McGivney.

He understood that communities become stronger when individuals take responsibility for one another.

The system he helped create simply gave that responsibility a structure.

Today the insurance profession continues that same mission on a broader scale.

When practiced with integrity, it allows millions of people to face life's uncertainties with greater

confidence.

So the question facing every professional is ultimately the same:

What standard will you carry forward?

Will the profession be practiced merely as a transaction?

Or will it continue to embody the spirit of mutual aid that inspired its earliest foundations?

The answer does not lie in institutions.

It lies in individuals.

In the quiet decisions made every day by those who guide families, protect businesses, and advise

communities.

If enough professionals choose to carry that spirit forward, the profession will never truly be forgotten.

It will simply be renewed by the character of the people who choose to serve within it.

And in that renewal, the promise at the heart of the profession will endure.

Closing Invitation

If this book has helped you in any way—whether it inspired you to pick up the phone, rebuild your confidence, or start fresh in your career—I'd love to hear from you.

Share your story. Tag me on LinkedIn: (www.linkedin.com/in/steven-wiatrek-a96492125)

Let me celebrate your success right alongside you.

You never know who your story might inspire next.

And if you're willing, send me a picture and a short note about how this book made a difference in your career. Who knows—your story might be the one I share next to encourage another agent to keep going when times get tough.

Invite Steven Wiatrek to Speak

If this book inspired you or your team and you'd like me to share these lessons in person, I'd be honored to speak at your next event. Whether it's an agency meeting, corporate leadership retreat, or industry conference, I focus on helping agents reignite purpose, sharpen skills, and build businesses that last.

My sessions aren't lectures—they're conversations. Real stories. Real lessons. Real results. I teach from the same heart that built this book: practical, personal, and proven.

Topics Include:
- Purpose-driven sales and service
- Old-school fundamentals that still win
- Rebuilding after setbacks (resilience and leadership)
- Community, legacy, and client loyalty

Universities & Community Colleges
I speak at no charge for universities and community colleges—all I ask is that travel is covered and books are purchased for students.

Bookings & Bulk Orders
To discuss speaking opportunities, collaborations, or bulk book orders, contact me at:
LinkedIn: linkedin.com/in/steven-wiatrek-a96492125
Email: swiatrek@gmail.com

Let's continue building a stronger, more inspired community of agents—one meeting, one story, and one success at a time.

"A single voice can ignite a spark, but a united message can light the world."

www.ingramcontent.com/pod-product-compliance
Lightning Source LLC
Chambersburg PA
CBHW051258130726
47987CB00004B/1570